Dedicated To My Lord Jesus Christ

And

To My Wife Karen,

The Wind Beneath My Wings

What They Are Saying About Chaplain Dave Fair's Book

This is a great idea, good tool, and great ministry piece. As we speak with folks from all over the world it would be good to have some thing like you book to encourage them so that first hand they could see what "Let Go and Let God" is all about. It is also a piece that could be used to help folks on the fence see why they should invest their dollars in Law Enforcement Chaplaincy.

Stu Nelson, Director of Marketing & Fundraising
International Conference of Police Chaplains

~

I love your book idea.

Dr. Judy Kuriansky
Adjunct Professor of Psychology
Columbia University Teachers College
New York Author and Talk Show Host

~

I am glad you have been able to put all your experience down on paper for others to benefit from it.

Rev. Wayne Whitelock, Chairman
International Conference of Police Chaplains
Disaster Committee

Congratulations, Dave!!

Rev. George A. Grimm, CTR (Ret.)

International Critical Incident Stress Foundation

(ICISF) Hotline/CISM Team Coordinator

~

Absolutely Awesome!

So real, fascinating, and intriguing!

Vaughn Donaldson, B.C.E.T.S.
Captain, Midland Fire Dept.
CISD Veteran- Midland, Texas
Oklahoma City, 911 Ground Zero, Jessica McClure Well
Rescue, Texas A. & M. Bond Fire

Mastering Law Enforcement Chaplaincy

Writings of Dr. David Fair from the first 15 Year's Chaplaincy

TABLE OF CONTENTS

Chaplain Dave Fair writing an article for ICPC Journal

Introduction

What does a police chaplain do?

"A police chaplain serves on two fronts," explains Dr. Fair. "On the one side, we provide chaplain services for police officers, civilian employees of a department, and police officers' families. This includes serving at a wedding, a funeral, in cases where is a death in the family, or any situation where there needs to be some psychological support."

"The other side is working with victims and people in the field that the officers come in contact with. Chaplains do death notifications. We provide counseling on family violence calls after the combatants have been separated and the threat removed. We get involved in cases of sexual assault, missing children, kidnappings and so on. We also frequently serve as a negotiator or a reference person in cases where there is a hostage or a barricaded subject. Chaplains attend almost every death scene that law enforcement is called to. Suicide prevention and intervention are other situations we get called in to help with."

Dave Fair, left, with Charles Figley, PhD, head of Green Cross Foundation, where Fair serves as a Board Member. Dr. Figley is known for his renowned work on Compassion Fatigue.

Photo taken during meeting of the Association of Traumatic Stress Specialist (ATSS) Board in Dallas, Texas April, 2005

BECOMING A CHAPLAIN

People frequently ask how I can become a Chaplain.

First one must realize a Chaplain is a minister of God, just like a church pastor or perish priest. There must be first and foremost a calling into the ministry of that person by God.

One can not just decide to be a Chaplain, anymore that one can wake up one morning and become a brain surgeon. There is a time of preparation, a time of training, and great sacrifice. There are several types of Chaplains, professional full time paid, professional part time paid, and volunteer.

Almost all professional paid positions require both a college degree and graduation from seminary. This alone moves most people toward the volunteer Chaplain positions.

Depending on the agency or institution one will be working with requirements for Chaplains vary. Some places require the same education for volunteers as that of professional Chaplains.

It should be noted that the term professional Chaplain does not mean paid Chaplains are any better than volunteers. It simply means that the Chaplain's profession is full time and that is his profession, how he makes his living. Volunteer Chaplains are usually bi-vocational.

There are no federal, state, or local Chaplain licenses. There are a number of organizations who offer various certifications in Chaplaincy. But the specific requirements of education and experience are usually set by the organization the Chaplain will be working for either as professional or volunteer.

In this day and time most institutions employing Chaplains want the minister to be the equivalent of a Licensed Professional Counselor (LPC), or something similar. Traditionally this requires a four year degree plus post graduate work. Normally a Masters or PhD. the equivalent in the ministry would be M. Div., D. Min., or a similar degree.

In addition to the degrees, most professional Chaplains are required to complete a minimum of four units of Clinical Pastoral Education (CPE). This involves working in a facility under the supervision of a Chaplain for usually one year. During this time the intern Chaplain is undergoing additional hands on training.

Volunteer Chaplains as a rule have not had CPE training.

In addition to the degrees and possible CPE, most institutions employing Chaplains also impose other requirements. Those are usually the requirements the Chaplain's own religious body mandates he or she meets to be sanctioned in Chaplaincy by their church. That usually is seen in the form of a written ecclesiastical endorsement from the religious body. In effect it guarantees the person is fit for Chaplaincy. In addition the Chaplain will be either ordained or licensed by his or her church.

Even as a volunteers, institutions are requiring much the same from volunteers as they do for full time paid Chaplains. This is due to both liability considerations and quality control of chaplain services.

In the health care field particularly hospitals, the Joint Commission requires Chaplains meet curtain criteria. This drives the requirements and you normally find at least one full time Chaplain supervising volunteer Chaplains.

For volunteer Chaplains there is a wealth of training that is very good but far less time consuming and less costly.

Chaplain Fellowship Ministries offers some excellent training and will assist you in starting your Chaplaincy work.

The Baptist General Convention of Texas offers a 9 week course, totaling 40 hours that includes 32 hours of general Chaplaincy training, 8 hours training in a field of specialty, such as health care, or criminal justice, followed by 6 months of supervised field training. This is excellent for volunteer Chaplains.

Upon completion the person becomes an approved Volunteer Chaplain. However this alone will not meet the requirements in most cases for Chaplaincy work in hospitals, jails, prisons, police agencies or similar locations.

The International Conference of Police Chaplains offers great training for law enforcement Chaplains through their regional and annual training sessions. The ICPC offers a Basic, Senior, and Master level certification.

Due to the variety of training and requirements in hospital settings a number of Chaplain organizations such as the Association Of Professional Chaplains, or The Association Of Clinical Pastoral Education offer certifications in health care Chaplaincy.

It is wise for a Chaplain volunteer, or professional to belong to one or more of these groups who specialize in training and certifying Chaplains in their area of specialty.

Certification by all groups has continuing education requirement each year.

So, "How Do I Become a Chaplain? " It should be clear from this article one must have a call and be willing to spend a lot of time and make a major commitment to the work. You may be volunteer as far as not being paid, but the demands and the joys are just the same as Professional Chaplains.

The best way to get started is to begin to pray for Gods leading and be sure of your call. Then check with local Chaplains in your community to find out about opportunities.

There are no short cuts to Chaplaincy. But for those who are called and equipped the satisfaction is tremendous.

Are Emotional Needs of Physical Trauma Victims Being Ignored?

Broken Bones May Be Set, But Wounded Souls Still Broken

As a Crisis Chaplain, I recently had a revelation. It came after comforting a critically injured patient and consoling his distraught family. As the helicopter lifted off taking the victim to a trauma center and his wife and daughter began the long 200 mile car ride, I couldn't help but wonder, what now? I knew the man's physical injuries would be addressed, but what about the injury to his soul. What about the psychological well being of his family.

Since the late 1980's much has been done to alleviate the emotional suffering of emergency service responders. In more recent years Critical Incident Stress Debriefing, Defusing and one on one, is being used in the private sector. Police, Fire, and EMS workers no longer have to hide their pain. Witnesses to school shootings, and mass disasters are being provided with psychological first aid.

Little is being said about meeting the same psychological needs of people who have been injured physically. It may be because we think hospital social workers are meeting the need. However after spending some 15 years as a Chaplain I know first hand these people's emotional needs are for the most part falling through the cracks. Social Workers have their hands full with logistics and paper work, and few referrals to psychologists or psychiatrists are being made.

It is not because no one wants to help people who have both physical and emotional scars. It's the old saying, "out of sight, out of mind ". Doctors order CT scans and MRI's, but there is no devise that can X-ray the soul. There may be some cursory comments made to the victim to breathe deep and relax, but there is usually no clear cut intervention to start the healing of the memories.

Of course there are priorities, start the breathing, stop the bleeding, and with the hustle and tussle of the emergency department there is little time for anything else before the next case comes along. Then with managed care the patient is hurried out of the facility in a few days to recuperate at home.

Speaking of home what about the family? They are dealing with the emotional turmoil of the injury, and possible life style changes. They may have been an uninjured party in the accident, or be dealing with the stress of thinking their loved one was going to die. We prepare family members of emergency workers in how to help their family deal with the psychological aftermath but what if anything is being done for the family of injury victims.

I have yet to see any discharge orders telling the patient what to do for their emotional well being. To be sure there are advocates who will see rape victims get the counseling needed, and victim service coordinators will frequently tell crime victims what's available. But for the trauma victim of a fiery car crash, a severed body part, or similar tragedy precious little is being done to relieve their emotional suffering. They are left to fend for themselves. The real shame comes when these people suffering from depression or a host of other ills stumble into a doctor or therapist's office with no idea of what has caused their problems. Like wise there is virtually no support of a psychological nature for family members.

A group of Texas Chaplains is developing a program called Emotional Recovery from Physical Trauma. (ERPT). The program incorporates a modified defusing technique, visual imagery, conversation medicine, and self-help to start the patient on the road to emotional heading while still in the hospital. It also addresses aftercare and help for the family. It is hoped the program will catch on, spread and spawn new ideas in an effort to heal the whole patient and help the family to facilitate the coping of the patient and themselves.

THE CALL FOR BACK UP

"AN ANALOGY THAT INVOLVES OFFICERS IN DEBRIEFINGS"

How many of us have had officers say, "Chaplain I don't need to attend a debriefing". We all know many times the "Macho" image of COPS can cause more harm then good. So many times officers don't want to attend a defusing or debriefing because they don't want to be perceived as weak or a cry baby.

There is a simple tool for your tool kit that will help get an officer to a debriefing. As a Chaplain simply say, " Bill have you ever responded to an officers call for back up? "Of course Bill will say yes. At that point the Chaplain can respond, "Bill, you would never withhold your help on a call for assistance from another officer would you? You would never hesitate to get involved in a battle if you needed to defend or save another officer would you?

What's the officer going to say? Naturally he would never fail to respond as a back up, he would give his life for a fellow officer. See the analogy? At this point you have the officer in the frame of mind for the next step.

"Bill, your fellow officers need you, they need your help and assistance. I know you may not need a debriefing (or defusing) but others do. That shooting (or death or whatever) was tough and trauma says pay me know or pay me later. Unresolved critical incidents can lead to health problems, substance abuse and divorce. Those other officers need your support, your input, and help. Will you attend the briefing and back them up? Be there for them? "

99.9 % of officers at this point will agree to attend the debriefing when you help them see it in this light. A few minutes talking to officers one on one when a debriefing or defusing call goes out will help get them in the meeting. Simply helping them to see their participation as needed back up will go a long way.

Chaplains Are Like a Box of Chocolates- A Variety of Fillings

The ambulance pulls into the ER and a critical patient is wheeled into the emergency room. A team of trauma physicians hovers around the lifeless figure. The admitting desk sees the situation and pages the Hospital Chaplain.

The Chaplain quickly responds and works with the arriving family of the victim. Information is carried back and fourth to those in the waiting area. The code is called. The Chaplain has to break the news.

Staying with the family. Papers to sign. Decisions to be made. Chaplain returns home to a cold dinner removed hours prior.

Who is this Chaplain? Or more correctly what is this Chaplain? Professional Chaplain, Community Clergy. Both?

Much is said today about the "Professional Chaplain". Two degrees and CPE. Ego wall in the office, parking space at the door.

Then the community clergy. Local minister's, who pastor churches, teach at universities, laity with the blessing of their faith tradition. They visit the sick, say prayers, and conduct funerals.

Enter a third breed. The trained and credentialed Chaplain. Yet maybe bi vocational, maybe splitting time between several parishes. Any less "professional"?

These Chaplains in many cases go where angels fear to tread. Found usually in smaller facilities, in tiny or rural communities hundreds of miles from metropolitan areas. Facilities with no Chaplain or spiritual care budget. Nada!

Yet these dedicated individuals have spent countless hours in both educational settings and training seminars, spending their own money, on their vacation time to quality themselves to serve in a no man's land.

These men and women have filled the need of hospitals and hospices alike and brought professional pastoral care and comfort to thousands. Many have been at it for years, availing themselves of teleconferences, books, papers, videos, and the Internet.

Yet in some circles these valiant servants are deemed less than "professional". After all they are not full time, that may have substituted formal C.P.E. by working with an experienced Chaplain arm in arm. They may not have been able to meet the specific legal requirements of curtain certifications from national associations, yet they have complied many times over in spirit.

Smaller medical settings are learning the term "Professional Chaplain", simply means the person is usually full time making their living at Chaplaincy. It is their chosen profession.

There are other Chaplains…. "Not of this fold", who because hospitals can't afford them have filled the gaps of spiritual care for years as volunteers.

Though volunteers these Chaplains are trained, experienced on the job, and above all do no further harm. They are considered hospital staff and part of the health care team. They chart, serve on committees, and respond all hours of the day and night. The joint commission and HIPPA recognize them as employees of the facility.

These men and women too are "Professional Chaplains "Professional in their approach and professional in the way they do there job. Maybe they should be called Expert Chaplains, that's another word for professional.

A lot of these Chaplains become experts, specializing in curtain types of care and intervention tailored to the needs of the facility. It may be suicide intervention, critical incident stress debriefing, ethics, or any number of needed disciplines.

Most also serve in the community as clergy. They are a "blend" of the school of hard knocks and education and training. Most of all they have earned the respect of the medical staff. The term professional can not be demanded. It must be earned.

Some have spent their time and money studying end of life and palliative care issues. Others are grief specialists or bereavement counselors.

There is a need for a word to describe this type of Chaplain. Adjectives such as dedicated, helpful and loyal fit, just fine. This new breed of Chaplains is professional in the truest since of the word.

Dignity in Death As Well As Life, SIDS

"He can not return to me, but I shall go to him"

I knew the call was going to be bad. I had been monitoring the EMS frequency between the ambulance and the emergency room when my pager had sounded. "Chaplain they are bringing in a possible SIDS".

The ambulance beat me to the ER, and when I entered the trauma room there intubated on the gurney was a little girl less than three months old. A frantic mother was just inside the room over come with grief. The E.R. Doc had called the code.

"We don't even have pictures of her", the mom sobbed. I held her in my arms and let her grieve, invaluable to help the healing begin.

The young father arrived. We were in the family room now and together the couple shed their tears. "We want to remember her life" the father said, "but we don't even have any pictures of her."

While the social service worker stayed with the couple I slipped up to the O.B. floor. I had recently heard about the Precious Memories program OB offered to parents of stillborn infants, and maybe we could use the concept for SIDS.

The OB supervisor concurred the program could be adapted for the SIDS baby, so the two of us accompanied by another OB nurse went to ER.

The first battle would be the tube in the infant. State law requires an autopsy and the tube is suppose to stay in place. The E.R. Doc bought into our effort and decided the tube would be removed

We then set about clipping locks of hair, and foot printing the infant for the memorial book.

Now it was time for pictures. I explained to the parents what we were doing. Thrilled there would be some recorded memory of their daughter they came with me to the trauma room.

There wrapped in her new blanker was their tiny daughter. The mother didn't hesitate picking her up. We took several photos of each parent with their child, then a final picture as a family.

With the parents resting back in the family room, we surveyed our work. In the memory book were pictures of the child, several locks of hair and, the footprints. In a small box rested the new baby blanket and little bonnet we used in the photos.

Words cannot express the look on the parents face when presented with the memories of their daughter. Still in shock several hours after the code had been called, they now had something concrete to cling to for years.

The funeral home arrived for the child; the parents said their tearful goodbyes. We exchanged phone numbers and they departed.

As I turned to thank the OB nurses we were all in tears. Mixed tears. Tears of sadness, yet tears of joy. We had been allowed to share in these scared moments of a young family, who now thanks to the care of two nurses and a little ingenious thought, have their future sacred moments on the pages of a little book and the contents of a small box.

Father Knows Best: Give God's Way a Chance

I was recently reading through several books ordered on Post Traumatic Stress Disorder and its treatment. I was looking at the various therapies we use to bring relief from the intrusive symptoms.

As I read and pondered I realized God had done some pretty good work in equipping the human body to heal itself. It only makes sense the mind can also heal.

Through out modern times we have become preoccupied with removing symptoms of illness and disease. The fever, the cough, the runny nose. We do all this without giving a thought to the fact some of these symptoms are allowed by God to facilitate the healing process.

It always puzzled me why the doctor would say, your chest is congested, the cough may break it up. Then he prescribes cough suppressant.

With some injuries we are told to stay off our feet for 24 hours. And we get better with rest.

Why did Mom say, go to bed early you'll feel better in the morning, and I almost always did.

Let's extend this logic and see what happens in curtain kinds of trauma, traumatic grief for example.

As a Chaplain I frequently have to deliver the worst news a family member will ever receive. "I'm sorry to tell you there has been an accident and your husband was killed".

One of the first things that happen to the poor sole receiving the news is shock and denial. We know this puts the person's psyche in neutral so they can take in the information a little at a time. If they didn't have this God given mechanism in place, they may be over come physically by grief. Literally they could die of a broken heart.

If we as counselors, or therapists attempted to remove shock and denial, we would be doing a great disservice to that person.

In my early years of Chaplaincy at a local hospital when a grieving widow would be wailing and throwing herself over the body of her deceased husband, I used to try to shut down her tears and wailing.

Why? Because it was uncomfortable to me, and caused staff and patients in ear shot to be uncomfortable.

We have long known tears are healing. God gave us the ability to cry. Studies have shown tears flush poison chemicals from the system. When we attempt to shut down a grieving person, we are interrupting God's grieving process.

Having looked at these examples let's consider some of the things that happen when a person is dealing with trauma.

Not wanting to go near the site of a trauma for fear of a trigger is common. Is that bad? Should we rush to help the victim become desensitized to curtain stimuli? Maybe not. Just maybe the desire to stay away is God's gift to them, much like shock. Later they can go near the scene a little at a time, much like desensitizing work.

Should we encourage a person to talk about a trauma immediately? Maybe not. The World Trade Center tragedy showed us much more harm than good would have been done, had we pushed firemen and police officers into full-scale interventions early on. Simple one on one conversation seemed to bring relief without doing further harm.

There is a problem with cookie cutter approaches to virtually any intervention. People are different. They like different colors, different foods, and modes of dress. To say one size fit's all is an absurdly. In our rush to do something, anything, maybe we are derailing the God given ability to heal ourselves.

What's the old saying? "Don't just stand there, do something ". What would happen is we did nothing for a change. Let the mind begin to heal.

I think maybe old Dr. Pete Walker our family friend and physician knew something when he would tell my panic stricken mom. "Give him two aspirin and call me in the morning"

Maybe Doc knew something we didn't or have forgotten. Sometime things are better left alone, at least for now.

I developed a minor health problem some time back and knowing the treatment I asked the doctor if he was going to prescribe something for me. He replied, not unless it becomes symptomatic. Only if the symptoms start causing a problem.

We are taught to do no further harm, and would do well to remember sometime the best help is doing nothing.

Am I saying brief interventions or counseling don't have a place? Of course not.

But as a preacher friend once said, "In my services, I don't always dump the whole load just because I prepared it.

The body will heal cuts and bruises. Broken bones will mend. Sprains and strains will repair on their own. Then it's reasonable to think the mind can also heal itself. For example we know dreams are a natural way for the desensitization process to begin.

Let's not be so quick to jump into someone's trauma and think we have all the answers. My Dad used to teach me, to stop, look, and listen before I did anything else. Maybe it's time we returned to some of our parent's advice.

The Bible says not to worry about today; tomorrow has enough trouble of its own. When in doubt, taking a wait and see attitude at least for today is not a bad idea.

I'll Cry for Her with You"

"Angels Unaware"

It was a really bad accident. There were three people brought in by ambulance. The two trauma rooms were full, and the cast room was also pressed into service.

The young women, a traumatic code didn't make it, the ER physician had called the code a short time after the ambulance and paramedics arrived.

It appeared the other two women might make it.

My task now working with the police. Notify the next of kin. The charge nurse handed me a driver's license from the belongings of the deceased. It listed her address in Midland, Texas.

Directory assistance in Midland gave a phone number, there was no answer. It was midnight and perhaps if she had family they too were gone.

After chatting with the ER doctor about the dilemma, I contacted the highway patrol office and asked them to have their trooper check the scene for other identifying information. There was none.

It occurred to me we might find some of the women's neighbors on the internet. The ER doctor went with me to the doctors' lounge where there was a computer and internet connection. Pulling up Midland and a search vehicle give me addresses. By entering the women's address the program gave a listing of neighbor's names and address.

Before we could get any farther the ER paged me to return. There stood a distraught young couple, they had seen the car at the accident scene and thought the dead woman was their friend. Their description fit.

It appeared the only way we were going to get the woman identified for curtain and locate relatives was through this couple. I asked the husband if he was willing to view the body to make identification. He agreed. He prepared himself and stiffened as I pulled back the sheet on the gurney. There was a sigh of relief. It wasn't her.

Back in the doctor's lounge I called directory assistance and began to gather phone numbers for the neighbors in Midland.

"Sorry to call you so late, this is Chaplain Fair with Brownwood Regional Medical Center in Brownwood. Do you know your neighbor Sue Jones (not her real name)". The first man didn't know her. The second man did. She was divorced, the mother of two boys, and no he didn't know any relatives.

Finally on the fourth call a woman knew her and knew of a father in Houston. She gave me a name and I was able to obtain a phone number from directory assistance.

Everything you are ever taught in Chaplain Training is never making a death notification by phone. But at this point we were not 100% sure we had the right man. Any questions would arouse suspicion. If he were the father he would have to be told.

"Mr. Jones (not his real name) "I introduced myself. " Do you have a daughter Sue? Does she live in Midland? Do you know where she is now? Traveling? On her way to see you?

"Mr. Jones I have some very bad news. Is there anyone else with you? Your daughter? Good. Mr. Jones there has been an auto accident near Brownwood. Sue was in the accident. I'm sorry Mr. Jones but Sue has been killed. She is dead".

After a long pause. A muffled sob. Something else I couldn't make out and a woman crying in the background. Mr. Jones was back on the line with questions. I related what I could to him. He and his wife and daughter would be in Brownwood the next day. They wanted to see their daughter.

With the charge nurse we made arrangements for the woman's body to be taken to the small hospital morgue. It would be held until the next day when the family would identify the body and make arrangements.

I received a call the next morning from the hospital; the victim's family had arrived at the hospital, would I meet them in the ER waiting room. Thinking to myself why the ER. The body was in the morgue.

After entering the ER, the charge nurse led me to a treatment room. There in the room the nurses had placed the woman. She had been cleaned up and appeared as if she were only asleep.

"We couldn't let the family see her like she was", the nurse said. "We even warmed her with heated blankets so when they touch her she won't be cold"

I was awed. Here a group of busy ER nurses had retrieved the body from the morgue, cleaned her and warmed her and placed her in a treatment room to lessen the trauma of the grieving family.

The family positively identified the woman. They sat by her bed, they talked to her, touched and caressed her.

At last they were ready to go, a funeral home had been called. Teary eyed they thanked us again and again for what we had done for their daughter. "It will be easier for us now", the father said. "She looks so at peace"

When I turned to thank the nurses who had gone the extra mile to help the family begin their healing, they had already returned to work.

I marveled. Nurses who never met the family, never knew the woman, had cared enough to create a sacred moment, for family, themselves, and for me. Angels unaware!

Promotional Ideas for Public Safety Chaplains

Many Bill Board Companies Will Do This Free
Because They Need To Place Public Service Messages on Some of Their Boards

VERY IMPORTANT
TO ORDER USE THIS ID#: 687843b

VERY IMPORTANT
TO ORDER USE THIS ID#: 687841b

Notice Lamar Advertising Placed Their Log on the Signs
Along with the Chaplain Group's Name

It Was the Best of Times; It Was the Worst Of Times

Is NBC's ER Too Real?

Thursday February 22, a young woman drove her car in front of a speeding train in a desperate suicide attempt. However she lived and others were killed, and over 30 persons were injured. The accident brought out police, fire, EMS, hospital workers and a rush of media.

The action was a stirring on the scene recreation that would make disaster make-up artists green with envy. If the wreck weren't enough, it triggered flashbacks for Luka one of the young docs on the show and through the magic of video viewers were whisked back to his war torn native land as a bomb hit his home injuring his wife and child.

His wife died while he was giving his young daughter CPR for hours because he couldn't care for both of them. And of course he lost his little girl when he quit CPR out of exhaustion.

Oh by the way, we were treated to the full flash back, as the young doctor gave it as part of his confession to a Catholic Priest who was a dying patient in the hospital. As the Priest said a prayer for the doc he flat lined as he gave the amen.

Did I mention that Dr. Benton by radio guided Carter through a double amputation of a fireman's legs, because the rescuer was trapped under the train and he was bleeding out? And Carter had to do the amputations that Elizabeth had started because she fell getting out of a helicopter at the scene and went into labor at 24 weeks.

All this in a one hour show less time for commercials. It was a bit overpowering but I must say rather well done. The scenes were realistic and I thought to myself as I watched this would make a good training film. Not of how to necessary but it would make a good introduction to new and would be medics and police recruits

Some of the open chest shots in ER were very real and after a number of successful seasons of ER camera men have gotten as good on tricky angle shots as have the video guys on COPS. Matter of fact ER at times looks better that the TV documentary Life in the ER on one of the learning channels that's the real thing.

Now that I have reviewed the TV show, here is my real reason for writing. When is enough, enough for the public and for us the emergency workers? Can shows like this cause emotional trauma? If jury members can be affected and need intervention from viewing gory crime scene photos then the answer is yes.

Further more although the show is a great primer for emergency workers can it act as a trigger for past events eliciting flashbacks? Here again the answer is yes.

Now no one wants TV shows to go back to the stark days of ADAM 12 (ask your father to explain) or even the more recent hospital drama St. Elsewhere, but there should be a balance.

We could make lemon aide out of the lemon here by using the show to promote the benefits of Critical Incident Stress Debriefing and other interventions. Much like made for TV movies that talk about domestic violence or incest and at the end have a short video from an intervention or support group, shows like ER could educate the public about the various area of assistance for emotional trauma that are available.

Some fiction shows in recent years have written in a brief mention of CISD or maybe showed a scene from a debriefing. But better yet one of the CISD gurus like Jeff Mitchell could do a brief overview of critical incidents and then the screen could show the number of ICISF and give a website for help from a variety of groups.

Bottom line is the networks need to give those of us working with emotional trauma an opportunity to piggyback on specific episodes. And we need to jump at the opportunity to tell the public there is help available. Would this be a good project for the ICISF to undertake?

Least We Forget, Trauma Is In the Eyes of the Beholder

A Simple 5 Minute Intervention That Works

In the aftermath of The World Trade Center , Columbine, Wedgwood, and so many other man made tragedy's there is a tendency to always be looking for the " big one ". That major critical event. That's the one where we can wear our jackets with the words Police Chaplain. That's the acute trauma where there is lots of press and teams fly in from all over the country.

Critical Incidents will continue to happen; they will dominate the news, and take much of our time and resources.

In the hustle bustle of the busy world as trauma workers we must make sure we don't forget the "sub critical events". These are the ones by DSM-IV TR standards not reflecting the criteria for a major diagnosis.

Never the less these people have been traumatized by something that has indeed upset their psyche. Pastoral Counseling Chaplains will be more apt to catch and address these sub critical events when presenting in the office. But street Chaplains may overlook these haggard souls especially when encountered in the work a day world.

People with" sub critical event" needs carry a double edged sword. Not only do they need intervention to mitigate the emotions, if they don't vent, those same people will be more apt to explode when the big one comes along.

One thing coming out of the Ground Zero experience was the phrase "Ventilate and Validate" When workers at the scene had little time or inclination to do much else, a three to five minute focused chat helped.

People have used talking as a means of healing for many years. The modern day CISD and defusing are only a codification and packaging of concepts dating back centuries.

In the "wild west", cowboys sat around the campfire talking (venting) about their day. Other roughriders would chime in, "you know that same thing happened to me". (Validation).

Yet ventilate and validate goes back to Biblical times. The "confessions "talked about in the Bible was a way to ventilate as were the numerous lamentations of the Old Testament.

The Catholic Church has long known the benefits of "confession" as a means of catharsis.

In the military the use of ventilation and validation was widely used as soldiers sat around eating k rations and talked about their battles.

There is an interesting comparison of those military men who developed "soldiers heart" (a fore runner of PTSD) in World War II and those who developed PTSD in the Viet Nam war. Reports for the VA state men who returned to the US in ships have days and weeks to decompress by talking about their experiences to their buddies. Yet those who flew home following Viet Nam had precious little time to vent and thus many are haunted by their past to this day.

Ventilate and Validate is not new, it is simply a "moniker 'or name given to a conversation that has some structure. Just like brief therapy, brief conversation has its place in helping people cope.

I first became aware of the success of this concept in the early 1990's, when called as a Police Chaplain to Killeen, Texas. A crazed killer drove his truck through Luby's Cafeteria and then opened fire killing over 20 people including him.

Although we also used CISD with police officers, a form of ventilate and validate was used to "triage"people emotionally. There was a place for both interventions, although some 10 years later, better tools such as Management Briefings coined by the ICISF would fit better due to the number of people involved.

We have talked mostly about "critical events ", yet we must remind ourselves that sub critical events in many cases need to be dealt with.

A modified "V and V" is a quick way for people suffering sub critical events to let off steam and realize their experience is in fact normal.

This V. & V. takes from lessons learned from Killen, Ground Zero and the many other tragic situations that faced the nation. I have used a form of V. & V. with emergency services workers I have been honored to work with since the 1980's. It has proved successful hundred's of times.

Dr. Dan Chapman, mental health professional for our Brownwood Crisis Trauma Team gives V. & V. high marks having used it himself at ground zero.

The Sub Critical Event V and V format is simple and to the point. I modified the brief stand up intervention (now the Sub V & V) so it works well for those situations when emotional first aid is needed. This is still a simple conversation, but the specific questions have proven successful in guiding the discussion to provide improved coping ability.

The outline is simple:

(1) The person is asked what event happened to them.

(2) What's bothering them most about the event?

(3) How they believe they can best deal with their feelings about the event.

(4) Then validating the feelings, stressing anyone going through the same event would feel the same way.

This is a 3-5 minute standing up intervention that can reap big rewards. In the normal fast paced environment in which we live and work people won't sit still in many cases even for a defusing.

But when a 5 minute, Sub Critical Event "V & V" is used people usually walk away better than when first encountered. At the least no further harm has been done.

The Sub Critical Event V & V can also be a quick triage tool to determine if more intervention or a referral is needed.

By making sure we have this tool in our bag of tricks hopefully no one has to suffer from sub critical events without a means of escape.

No Easy Answers

Why Does God Let Bad Things Happen

As a Police Chaplain I am faced almost daily with death. Some death as in the case of the elderly may be expected. Doesn't make it any easier, just expected. Some death such as the traumatic death of a child comes without warning.

There are rapes, murders, horrendous auto accidents. All of this death and human suffering beg the question, why does God let these tragedies happen?

The question is much more magnified when asked with the backdrop of the terrorist acts in New York and Washington D.C.

Theologians have argued for years over these and other questions. Insurance Companies even call some catastrophic events "Acts Of God ".

When faced with the question of why a 5 year old is killed in an auto accident, or why a plane crashes, as a Chaplain I'm expected to have answers. In my own struggle of why bad things happen, I have drawn on Biblical text, and writings of much more learned people than I.

While not pretending to know it all, I have gleaned what I think are some basic truths that help us get a glimpse of understanding.

There are at least two basic laws or principals in force. First are the "natural laws ", things like the law of gravity. If I pick a book up from my desk and drop it to the floor, the law of gravity is in affect. It falls to the ground.

If bolts break and an engine or a wing fall off an airplane if can't fly. The law of gravity takes over and it falls to the ground.

If fuel and heat meet, a fire starts. Fires burn. Again a natural law. Fire can cause death and destruction.

If I am driving down the road and look away, and run into another vehicle, I have no one to blame but myself. If my wife is not wearing a seat belt and is thrown into the dash, the law of motion is in play.

The second law is the “Free will moral agency of man ". This means God has made men free to make their own choices. In the Garden of Eden, God told Adam and Eve not to eat of the tree. (Genesis 2: 16-18) They disobeyed God and made the choice to eat the fruit anyway.

God told them to make the right choice, but He did not stop them from making a bad choice. Thus we have the “free will “of man to choose.

In the Old Testament God said, I set before you today death and life. I want you to choose life. (Deuteronomy 30:19) Even though God told us what choice to make he leaves the choice to us. People every day make bad choices. They make tragic choices, but God does not interfere with those choices today anymore than He interfered with Adam and Eve.

He respects the right He has given us to choose.

The sad fact is when either of these two laws is in effect or a combination of the two people can die. In the aftermath of the terrorist attacks on the United States people ask where God was. The answer is God is right where He always is. He is right there with us showing us the right road to take. The correct choice to make. But He leaves that choice to man, and He grieves when we make the wrong choice.

We must remember there are dozens of outside influences affecting the choices man makes. It is the constant battle between good and evil, between light and darkness. But it is a choice. As God said, I set before you this day life and death, blessing and cursing. I want you to choose life.

One Size Doesn't Fit All

It's Time to Rethink Our Approach to Intervention in Emotional Trauma

My daughter recently bought a new car. It was green. She and her husband love green. I hate it! On vacation my wife likes to tour and shop. I like to lie on the beach! I have a granddaughter who likes green vegetables. I don't!

The fact is we are all different. God made us that way. The Bible even talks about it saying that everyone can't be a foot or a nose. We would look pretty funny.

We were all raised differently. Have different backgrounds and carry various baggages. Some of us are Type A personalities, some are laid back.

My point is we can not expect the same intervention strategies to work on everyone, every time.

A cookie cutter approach to crisis intervention no matter how well packaged simply isn't always the best we can do. Never the less many times we are still trying to do it. Like saying eat your veggies they are good for you.

There has been a good deal of press in recent years about the pro's and cons of Critical Incident Stress Debriefing. Is it helpful, hurtful, works, doesn't work? I think there is no question that CISD or one of the companion interventions works. But not on everyone every time.

There is a host of interventions with proponents pointing out not to confuse CISM with psychotherapy. There are defusings, debriefings, management briefings and a ton of other strategies.

The trick is to decide what to use, and when, if at all to use it. 911 shattered any belief that our normal interventions could be used without modification in the first days and even weeks after the buildings fell. I was at Ground Zero the week after the disaster struck and I saw people trying to use Critical Incident Stress Debriefing too soon.

I saw inappropriate attempts at intervention and trained clinicians trying to use office skills among the dirt and steel.

Questions we have to ask ourselves are "what do these people need, right now, today", "what do they not need", and who can provide it.

We can't simply take our training and try to say here try this on. Just because we were trained to follow a list of steps or a set procedure doesn't mean it will work every time, even on much smaller incidents than the World Trade Center.

CISM and similar approaches is not a "magic wand". I don't think those who first packaged the ideas ever intended them to be or said they were. Yet many folks just took off and ran like it was the panacea for every emotional trauma.

We must also understand that most CISM as taught today is not rocket science nor is it especially new. The concepts of CISD and related topics were not birthed in the 1980's but rather rebirth and packaged.

The military has a long history of similar use of some of these concepts. Mater of fact the whole idea of venting goes back years.

People have used talking as a means of healing for centuries. The modern day CISD and defusing are only a codification and packaging of concepts dating back years.

In the "wild west", cowboys sat around the campfire talking (venting) about their day. Other roughriders would chime in, "you know that same thing happened to me". (validation)

Yet ventilate and validate goes back to Biblical times. The "confessions "talked about in the Bible was a way to ventilate as were the numerous lamentations of the Old Testament.

The Catholic Church has long known the benefits of "confession" as a means of catharsis.

In the military the use of ventilation and validation was widely used as soldiers sat around eating "k" rations and talked about their battles.

There is an interesting comparison of those military men who developed "soldiers heart" (a fore runner of PTSD) in World War II and those who developed PTSD in Viet Nam. Reports from the VA state men who returned to the US in ships had days and weeks to decompress by talking about their experiences to their buddies. Yet those who flew home following Viet Nam had precious little time to vent and thus many are haunted by their past to this day.

One of the very first things I learned in my education and training with any intervention is to "do no further harm". There are a lot of things we can say that will re traumatize an individual. Yet there are a lot of things we can do correctly.

I'm reminded of the pictures especially from World War II and in the Viet Nam War nurses were simply sitting holding a wounded soldier's hand. Sometimes that is all they could do and sometimes that was all that was required.

When I first returned from Ground Zero, I was depressed for a number of reasons. One of the biggest was the feeling we did no good what so ever with the policemen, fire fighters and EMS workers on the pile.

After all what most of us did in the initial days was pause to chat briefly, offer our condolences over the loss of their friends, let them use our cell phone to call home, and place a hand on their arm or shoulder.

I was concerned that there hadn't been enough intervention. You know the real nuts and bolts of intervention. Guess I expected us to all be able to sit around in a circle and talk about the days happenings. Guess I expected it to be a text book case of introductions, first thoughts and the like.

I told a friend on my return, I didn't think we had helped anyone. All we did was mostly "hand holding". As I look back, now over a year later, as I read the reports and look at the surveys of how we as Chaplains and debriefers did, I see "hand holding "was just what they needed at the time.

It's hard to go wrong just holding someone's hand and letting them know you hear them and you care.

The whole picture has taken me back to my beginning Chaplain days. A wise old Chaplain in responding to a question of what to say when you didn't know what to say answered "say nothing". Just be there with the "ministry of presents."

The old adage is they don't care what you know, until they know that you care.

I was at a debriefing in a near by town a few years ago. I think it was over a horrible traffic accident. I had never worked with the person before who was going to lead the debriefing.

There she was with her text book and notes in hand, and a check list ready to go with the group of emergency workers. A "cookie cutter approach". Never mind what the group really needed. We were going to tell them what they needed.

It was like a doctor prescribing medicine without a history or exam. We muddled through and made it work, not because we followed the check list without deviation, but because we did a bit of "hand holding."

We can all write our checks, go to training, get our certificates and be ready to go, but if we leave common since at the door, the people we intend to serve will be better off if we don't come at all.

CISD and CISM will always have a place. There will always be more classes to take and more training to attend. But we have to remember, one size doesn't fit all.

I still don't like the color green! Not sure I ever will. But you know that's ok too. Because one size doesn't fit all and it shouldn't.

Reprogramming of Your Mind and Emotions

Following a Critical Incident

10 COMMANDMENTS FOR GETTING BETTER

It is important to know that with a little help you will recover from your Critical Incident. Normally within 4 to 6 weeks people are well on their way to recovery. Occasionally someone gets "stuck" and additional help is needed.

If you don't feel you are coming out of it in about 6 weeks you need to seek additional help. Failure to do so could allow your Critical Incident NORMAL reactions to turn into Post Traumatic Stress Disorder (PTSD) a much more serious problem.

Here are some things you can do to help speed your recovery:

(1) Talk..Talk..Talk.....talking about the incident is very beneficial. Talk in as much detail as possible. Describe the little things the way you saw them, what you heard, or even smelled. Talk is like washing a wound it cleans it, by talking in the open you will lessen the changes of nightmares and flashbacks of the event. When things are unresolved in your mind, you dream about them.

(2) Your body can't distinguish between what is really happening and what is an “instant replay “in your mind. Because of this when the events replay in your mind, you may get the same emotional and physical reaction you did during the actual event. This is because the adrenaline is kicking back into your body.

And that substance can be like leaving your car in park and floor boarding the gas. To burn off excess adrenaline exercise is helpful. It can be moderate. Walking is fine. 30 minutes a day of exercise will burn off the adrenaline and help relieve that “keyed up" feeling.

(3) Spend time with others, but make sure they are positive people. By being around others you have less time to just sit and think. The old

story that an idle mind is the devils workshop is true. When your mind is in neutral the thoughts of the incident will fill it. So being around positive people with healthy distractions can be helpful.. Remember you still want to talk about the event.

(4) Smoking and caffeine cause the system to react just like adrenaline. So consider cutting down on these during your recovery period. Lots of sugar and junk food also is not helpful. This is a time to try to eat decent balanced meals.

(5) Consider taking a good multi vitamin. It does not have to be a high dollar one, just a simple one a day vitamin is good. Stress depletes your system of vital vitamins.

(6) Don't complicate the critical incident by trying to cover up the feeling with alcohol or drugs. Stress says pay me know or pay me later. Dealing with it now, while it is fresh is best.

(7) Be aware of triggers. There are places you may go, people you may see, or TV or movies that may trigger intense feelings about the event. While you want to be careful that you don't get into avoidance behavior being careful for now about what you watch and read is important. The wrong things can stimulate the nervous system.

(8) Drink plenty of water. Eight glasses a day. It’s as simple as that

(9) Don't make any major life changing decisions during the 4 to 6 weeks after the incident. Impulse control may be weak and you may do something you will regret later.

(10) If it’s been a while since you have spent some time with God now is a good time to do some Bible reading. Psalms is a good place to start.

IF YOU BEGIN TO EXPERIENCE THESE THINGS PTSD COULD BE TRYING TO TAKE HOLD SEEK PROFESSIONAL HELP

Disturbing memories of the event come to mind without warning

Continued nightmares about the incident

Feeling like the event were happening again

Psychological distress around the anniversary of the event

Avoiding thoughts or feelings about the incident

Avoiding activities that recall the event

Loss of memory about major aspects of the event

Loss of interest in activities previously enjoyed

Trying to numb your emotions

Feeling detached from others

Loss of loving feelings toward others

Sense of shortened future

Difficulty in falling and staying asleep

Intense irritability

Difficulty concentrating

Startle reflexes

Excessive suspicion and caution in dealing with others

Feeling keyed up and unable to relax

Loss of most emotional control

Experiencing a few of these things may be normal. When you begin to experience a number of them especially after the 4 - 6 week healing period then there may be cause for concern and professional help should be sought.

Chaplain Cumulative Stress Syndrome

Why the Chaplain Needs a Chaplain

Last year when a close Chaplain friend and I both suffered a period of Panic Attacks, we thought it strange. Later when we both went through a time of being withdrawn it began to become apparent something was wrong. Why both of us, why the same symptoms.

All we need today is another buzz word. But Chaplain Cumulative Stress Syndrome is very real, and unlike a specific Critical Incident a debriefing is not the answer.

CCSS is a combination of Critical Incidents that do not have time to resolve and the accumulation of stressors that come from seeing first hand the day to day trauma on the streets and then having to be a shock absorber for the other trauma officers see.

In short the Chaplain tends to "Gunny Sack", all his own and everyone else's emotional garbage. When not emptied on a regular basis the "Gunny Sack", becomes so full the most "minor" incident can cause it to rip open spilling its ugly contents all over everything and everyone in the path.

While Critical Incident Stress Debriefings are excellent they have a specific purpose and are used to address a one time major incident that has taken the participants beyond the range of normal human emotion.

CCSS starts as a tiny splinter under the skin, and if not addressed becomes a full blown issue that forms infection effecting the rest of the body ultimately forming scar tissue that is difficult if not impossible to remove.

Several years ago while serving as a City Councilman (and a Chaplain) our community were faced with the Ku Klux Klan coming to town for a major demonstration. Because of legal issues the council was unable to deny a permit for the rally. The result was a very trying time that pits much of the community against one another.

In desperation I tried but all my normal coping resources failed to work. Then I hit on the idea of talking to another of our Police Chaplains about the matter. The result was miraculous. The Lord had used this Chaplain to ease my burden and given me some valuable insight.

It wasn't rocket science it was simply recognizing I had a problem and swallowing enough pride to go talk to a peer. When we began to talk I quickly realized the rally and permit controversy were not the only issue.

Not long before I had spent four days in Killeen, Texas debriefing police and EMS following the Luby's Massacre. In addition by spending about 16 hours a week in a patrol car with officers and hearing their pain coupled with the actual incidents I saw on almost a daily basis something had to give.

I wasn't able to put a name on it then, but today it is very clear that it was Chaplain Cumulative Stress Syndrome. They key to understanding the syndrome is knowing that the Chaplain is both a primary victim and a secondary victim.

Sometimes both from the same incident. The best analogy of this would be a car wreck. You are in your car and someone runs into you (the primary accident) then several other vehicles pile into that accident (secondary). Maybe your vehicle could stand up to the first impact but by the time the additional pile up occurs your vehicle is ready for the scrap yard.

Then add to the load most Chaplains have a congregation and with the usual matters that come from Pastoral duties the plate is pretty full. The burn out rate for conventional ministers is high, so imagine the burden a Police Chaplain is carrying with no place to dump the emotional trash. This is not to discount Gods help. We know to cast our cares upon Him because He cares for us. But fact is sometimes, we need someone to help us lift the trash can.

As Chaplains we don't usually have the luxury of passing it on. Because of confidentiality and other factors we must become "shock absorbers", and those wear out after a time. Now enter the Chaplains

Chaplain, the man (or women) who is going to help us take the twist tie off our "Gunny Sack" and get it dumped.

Call them what you will Trauma Relief Chaplains, Stress Reduction Chaplains, or Peer Chaplains the name doesn't matter. The fact is we need to give some training to Chaplains who at a peer level will Chaplain the Chaplains.

How would it be best to get a beleaguered Police chaplain on the road to healing? One suggestion is an intensive weekend retreat where the Chaplain needing to recharge is teamed with a Peer Chaplain as a roommate. Informal instruction could be offered during the mornings to those Chaplains seeking the beginning of a healing. A private time for all in the afternoon with the evening devoted to in room one on ones between the paired Chaplains.

The key to success in this program is proper training of the Peer Chaplain who must first have been through the program him or herself and then it is critical that one on one time be spent. After the Chaplains are paired. In addition follow up between the Peer Chaplain and the other Chaplain is necessary. The healing Chaplain should be able to call upon the Peer Chaplain to help him walk through the remainder of the process.

A Sample Weekend Retreat Might Look Like This:

Police Chaplain Stress Reduction Seminar

Saturday

8 AM - Noon - Seminar
Noon- 1:00 PM- Lunch
1:00 - 4:00 PM- Private Quiet Time
4:00 - 6:00 PM- Free Time
6:00 - 7:00 PM Dinner
7:00 – 9:00 PM in Room One on One

Sunday

8:00 - 9:00 AM Breakfast

9:00 -Noon - Training Group
Noon - 1: 00 PM Lunch
1:00 -4:00 PM in Room One On One
4:00 PM Check Out

The training session would deal with coping with the stress and trauma, while the one on ones would involve intense sharing by the burdened Chaplain to the Peer Chaplain. This is the meat of the program. The quiet time of course would be for Bible, inspirational reading, and prayer on an individual basis.

The other hurdle is how to train the Peer Chaplains and this is where I will begin to end this article. I propose the ICPC name a committee to study this concept and begin to come up with Peer Chaplain Training. Going even so far as offering a Peer Chaplain certification.

Look around you how many Chaplains do you know who started a work and are no longer in the active Law Enforcement Chaplaincy? What happened to them? In our program in Brownwood, Texas 10 years ago we started with 15 Chaplains, two additional men were phased in along the way. But from a total of 17 today only 5 remain. Think about it.

In case we have forgotten we are flesh and blood just like the other guy, we bleed, we hurt, we get burned out, we get ill, and sometimes we die before our time. It is my belief that a Peer Chaplain Program with training and retreats can reduce Chaplain Cumulative Stress Syndrome thereby saving ministries, ministers, and families all to the Glory of God.

SWORD AND SHIELD

As we go through this life there are many joys and sorrows. They come with the territory. As a Police Chaplain I get to deal with mostly the sorrows of life and see people at their worst.

When their guard is down. I see them as they are where the rubber meets the road. When tragedy strikes people are looking for answers and for comfort. My job is to help them find the answers and as best I can give comfort.

Usually my contact with people is in the form of a serious injury or death of a loved one. Most often it's delivering the devastating news of the death. Responses vary but they almost always include even for the most non religious person questioning God.

I have found the answers and comfort both come from the same place, Gods Word, the Bible. The Bible and its application, in finding answers and giving comfort to hurting people is a real tool. The Bible is full of examples of people who have numerous questions about the circumstances and experiences of extreme tragedy.

From Adam and Eve who first tasted of the apple and reaped the consequences of the first sin to Jesus himself who endured the Cross, man has suffered and questioned why. Thus the old adage, Why Me Lord?

Jesus asked, from the Cross Father why have you forsaken me? And Cain when marked and driven away told God that his punishment was too much to bear.

This was after he asked God following his murder of Able, "Am I my brother's keeper"? The Bible tells us to "Cast our cares upon Jesus, for He cares for us" My job as Police Chaplain is to help victims find practical ways to do just that.

The Brownwood, Texas Police Chaplain Program began in 1988 under the direction of then Police Chief Joe Don Taylor. The 24 original Chaplains have dwindled to 5. Chaplains like anyone else are subject to stress and burnout and over the years it has taken its toll on the local Chaplain program.

Chaplains go through much the same training as law enforcement officers, wear uniforms, and ride with the officers. When trouble comes resulting in emotional, physical, and spiritual unrest the Chaplain is there to lend a helping hand.

Pounding a person over the head with the Bible, quoting numerous scriptures, or regressing to "church speak", are of no real help when tragedy strikes. The ministry of presence, just being there for the hurting and providing practical help is the real asset, a Chaplain has if he wants to be effective.

They may not remember what you say but they will remember you were there for them. I have called other relatives for them, held their hand, notified the funeral home and provided a glass of water. What ever the need, the Chaplain tries to provide.

This is not to say there is no place for spiritual things. Certainly there is. It may be a prayer, or even being asked to preach a funeral.

All through the Bible Jesus helped in practical ways. The commentaries on the various books of the Bible chronicle almost step by step the journey taken over thousands of years of strife, grief and pain man had endured. The books on the lives of many Bible characters add flesh, blood and a dimension of reality to the Bible.

We find that even men such as King David were human and experienced sin, weakness, and trauma. David committed adultery then ordered the husband of the woman to be placed on the front lines of battle so he would be killed.

He then married the woman and she had a child. However the child died and David is seen going through intense mourning. The Prophet Nathan comes to David and gives a chilling tale of a man who commits adultery and murder. David realizes it is he the prophet speaks of and as a result many Psalms in the Book of Psalms were penned. So out of tragedy we see that success can come.

Sometimes life's most positive lessons are learned in not so positive ways. The death of Jesus on the Cross was first seen by many as a defeat for Jesus and His followers, yet the death, burial, and resurrection are the corner stones of the Christian faith. Without the endurance's of Jesus at Calvary, and His death and what appeared to be sure defeat the world would not have Christianity today.

A good minister does not necessarily a good Chaplain make. Ministers, pastors, elders, and deacons, all work in a controlled environment. The Chaplain for the most part works in the field, where the rubber meets the road. What works inside the stained glass window will not necessary work outside? This is particularly true of "church speak", and canned stoic like phrases.

Even a devout church goer is seldom comforted by just quoting scripture alone. It has been said that a minister can be so heavenly minded he is no earthly good. When ones halo is on too tightly there is little or no chance of real ministry. People don't want to know what you know until they know that you care.

The phases of grief are

- shock
- denial
- bargaining
- depression
- acceptance.

Fact is they don't necessary go in order and they skip around and back and forth. In the bargaining with God phase, it is usually said, God I will do this if you will let them be OK, not be dead or a host of other deals one tries to make.

God is not a slot machine, but it is OK for people to go through the stages. Matter of fact it is essential a person go those all stages of grief if they expect an emotional healing to begin.

Once in an emergency room at a hospital, a woman was clinging to the body of her dead husband. She was crying and wailing. I was trying without success to help her stop. It was the worse thing I could have done to her. I was trying to shut her down not for her benefit but because I was very uncomfortable with the scenario.

She needed to cry, needed to vent. But I was more than willing to say there, there Mrs. Jones, it will be all right he is in a much better place. This is not what a person needs or wants to hear. Pat answers are useless. They may satisfy our need to say "something" anything. However they can do ever lasting harm.

Some of the catch all one lines are:

- "God needed another little flower in heaven". It's a lie, God has all the flowers He needs or wants. He is the great Creator. The Bible says He owns all the cattle on a thousand hills. He didn't need to take someone's three year old.
- "There you can have more children", or the ever popular "You have other children" That's like telling an amputee, there you

have another leg. How absurd. A loss is a loss is a loss. And must be grieved as such. It doesn't matter how many children a person has each one is a unique individual.

- "They are much better off now". This is tricky. The fact is the dead relative if a Christian will indeed be in a better place. But to those left behind the best place is here with them. A minister who tosses this to a family member simply tosses guilt. The survivor is thinking well Aunt Jane is in heaven. But I'm mad God took her. Then they feel guilty because they are mad at God.

By the way, God has big shoulders. It's ok to be mad at Him. After all anger is an emotion He gave us. The Bible says, "Be angry and sin not, don't let the sun go down on your wrath".

This makes it clear from a Biblical perspective we are apt to be mad, the sin is staying mad, day after day. Misplaced anger may even be directed at a Chaplain. That's why I never go on a death notification alone.

I hate to think of a surviving family member who has no hope and no one to lean on. A person who had never had an encounter with the Living Christ, how very alone that person must be. It would be tragic for me to not be able to say, lets pray, or cast your care upon Jesus along with practical appropriate remarks. How would I be able to help as a Chaplain if there were no God, no Jesus, for than matter no Bible?

The sad truth is there are none of these. They do not exist to a person who doesn't know the Lord. The Bible and books about the Bible help us flesh out our faith as Chaplains and laymen along the road we trod.

We Are Our Brothers Keeper:

Don't Forget the Partners of Fallen Officers During Police Memorial Week

"I know exactly what my partner is going to do on any given call". Those are the words of a police officer, about his partner. "We think and react the same way", says another officer about his partner.

Ask any spouse, police partners are tight, tighter in fact than some marriage partners. That leads to its own problems, but that's another story.

In working with officers who have been involved in shooting incidents, officers who have been shot, and making officer family notifications Chaplains as well as the department tend to focus on the downed officer, if wounded, and the officers family if he is wounded or killed.

Almost every department protocol I have seen in some 15 years of law enforcement Chaplaincy has very specific details for the officer's family concerning where to walk, where to sit, and where to ride.

The fact is there is a forgotten family member in every police fatality. The partner of the slain officer. It is no secret law enforcement is a sub culture all its own. And buried deep in that culture is a clear understanding of the law enforcement family. That family is thicker than blood, as the saying goes.

To leave the officers partner out of support at the hospital when his partner is injured or slain, to leave him or her out of funeral plans, to leave him out of after service support, and even trips to the National Police Memorial is as bad as leaving out a spouse or child.

Police partners are re traumatized enough by reliving the incident for the investigators, testifying at trial, and seeing all the media coverage. Then to not include them as part of the family can be devastating.

The Chaplain is in an important place to make sure the law enforcement partner is not left out. It may be conveyed by talking to the chief, the officer liaison, or even to the surviving police spouse.

Remember too that the partner is grieving and in need of the same support as a traditional family member. Departments should allow a partner time off just as you would an officer who had lost a spouse.

It is common knowledge that officers throughout a department will be affected by the death of a fellow officer. Most if not all will grieve, but no one will take it as hard as the slain officer's partner. As Chaplains we need to stand in the gap and connect the dots so partners will be involved as well as get the support they need in their time of sorrow.

"When Do I Earn My Own Wheels"

A look at the pros and cons of the Chaplain Having a department vehicle

I remember as a kid I got my drivers license when I turned 16, but it was a long time before I got my own car. To top it off when I had my first car I had to run errands for Mom and cart little brother around. Sometimes I wondered how good a deal I got.

When I first joined the police Chaplain Program some 13 years ago I was awed by getting to ride-a-long with the officers. I loved the adrenalin rush and the opportunity to minister to those in need. Some of my most awesome moments in ministry came in the front seat of the patrol car.

As I attended more ICPC training and gained experience I began to assist the officers on family violence calls, death scenes, and attempted suicides. Seems many times I felt rushed to finish what I was doing with a survivor or family member. The officers business there might be finished but mine was just getting started.

There were other calls holding, or it was shift change. Most of the time the officer couldn't stay with me and if he left me it might be hours before another unit could break loose to give me a ride.

What to do. I tried responding in my own vehicle at times, but crime scene restrictions, and crowded streets with emergency vehicles make it next to impossible.

Finally I spoke to the Chief about the use of a department patrol vehicle. If the Chaplain has his own department car he could come and go at will.

While he was sympathetic to the Chaplains plight he had a concern. His problem with the Chaplain driving a police car was a citizen in trouble flagging the car down expecting to find a police officer.

We struck a compromise. A local sign company made some large magnetic signs saying POLICE CHAPLAIN. One set stuck to each door and another was placed on the rear. This gave us the ability to convert a patrol vehicle to a Chaplain car in 30 seconds with no damage to the vehicle.

This program was implemented for six months. It became clear the Chaplain having an official vehicle to respond in was a great asset to the department.

The one problem was what happened when all the cars were being used for patrol and there was no spare vehicle? Many times one or more police cars were in the shop. This left the Chaplain either afoot or back in the patrol car with the hurried officer.

At long last a solution was reached. When it came time to trade in patrol vehicles the Chief and City Manager agreed to hold back the best trade in for fulltime assignment to the Chaplain Unit. The city was only getting about $2,000 in trade and even if a car had 100,000 miles it would be fine for routine response use by the Chaplain.

The car was cleaned up and detailed. The light bar and radio were left and new carpet installed. In addition the words in red CHAPLAIN were added to both sides and the trunk of the car. Along with the standard police markings the car was clearly marked Chaplain, but still retaining its official look.

The program has worked well. We have three Chaplains in our department. We each take several duty days in a row. This allows us to keep the vehicle in our possession. In addition the Chaplain is allowed to take the vehicle home so he can respond in it after hours.

One of the benefits of the Chaplain vehicle is it increases police visibility on the streets. Chaplain's don't use the emergency lights when in motion but can use them when parked at an accident scene. There are times an officer will ask the Chaplain to block an intersection with the Chaplain car to free the officer up to investigate.

While the use of our own vehicle solved many problems it could potentially create a new one. We did not want to be cut off from ridding with the officers. That was an important part of the Chaplains ministry.

In answer to that potential problem, the Chaplains who are not on call, frequently come in and do ride-a-longs with the officers. The on duty Chaplain still has the Chaplain vehicle and carried out his duties. The best of both worlds.

Insurance and liability considerations must be addressed by the city. Early on the Chaplains were listed as city employees. Although not compensated, this was done for workers comp and liability insurance reasons. Chaplains had already been allowed to drive department vehicles in a pinch or on out of town trips.

A creative city attorney and city manager can work out the details and the little cost to the city is far offset by the increased police presence and the additional things a Chaplain with a car can do. It is sort of like being 16 all over again.

"Chaplain can you pick up the meals for the prisoners? Chaplain can you drop this juvenile off at home? Chaplain I have a flat on my unit. Can you pick me up?

The Columbia Shuttle Recovery…

"Their Mission Has Become Our Mission"

"Their mission has become our mission" the mantra of thousands who searched east Texas looking for remains of the Space Shuttle Columbia. Coming apart, falling to earth February 1, 2003 in thousands of pieces, all seven astronauts perishing.

The second largest city in Navarro County Texas became the Incident Command Post of Corsicana. 1,100 people weekly call the warehouse complex home. They sleep there, shower there, and except for a brown bag lunch for the field, eat there. Hundreds of tents form lines in buildings. Remember don't slam the screen door after 22:00 hours, they try to sleep.

East Texas became the initial resting place for remains of the astronauts and space shuttle. The astronauts have gone home; most of the shuttle has not.

During the first few days local residents and law enforcement combed hills, and fields assisting in recovery. Yellow evidence tape among the greening grass. Days turned into weeks.

FEMA funds the recovery program under the direction of NASA. Daily thousands of forest service fire fighters, Bureau of Land Management staff, contract hires and even Native American Indians are walking ten feet apart, looking. A hand full of NASA employees, personal friends of the Columbia Crew search with them.

My first contact with ICP Corsicana was a few days after an e-mail from Paul Tabor coordinator of the Texas Department of Health, Bureau of Emergency Management, Critical Incident Stress Management Network.

I head a state network local team. The State Crisis Consortium including Texas Department of Mental Health and Mental Retardation wanted two CISM trained persons at each of the six Texas incident command locations spread throughout the state.

Arriving early Saturday morning to begin my tour wondering if experience as a CISM trained Police Chaplain had prepared me for the task ahead.

Clearly reminded by state, CISM is not therapy, do only interventions. Engage workers in conversation, let them vent.

My first encounter was a young NASA security guard from Kennedy Space Center in Florida. He volunteered for assignment in Texas. Twelve hour shifts guarding recovered parts.

Yes he knew the crew. He was off duty when Mission Control lost contact with Columbia. Like hundreds of others he couldn't believe it was happening. He wanted to be in Texas, guarding shuttle debris.

My first day at camp I visited with as many people possible. Trying to get the lay of the land, how the command structure worked,
Who walked out the grids, what made the operation tick.

Part of my answer came during orientation. Three men are still in the space station above earth. Another shuttle would not be launched to supply the station or bring them home until the problem causing the Columbia disaster was found and fixed.

Every man and woman involved in the recovery effort, those walking the grids, cooking, doing laundry, issuing rain gear, all operations, all support, all were involved in bringing the Columbia and her crew home. The Columbia crew's mission had become our mission.

All of us were involved in helping the space shuttle program go forward. We all were playing a part. Each of us was part of history.

Meeting ICP command, human services, logistics and medical. The medical operation caught my eye and heart.

Medical was manned by emergency medical personal, some local, some from as far as Wyoming. They had a medical tent and three vans in the field checking on crews. It stood to reason anyone having problems with stress could end up with the medics.

Making the medical tent my unofficial base of operations, I asked the team leader's permission to go with the medics. The request was approved. "They leave at 7:00 AM tomorrow", she said.

Leather Warden an Associate Police Chaplain made the trip with me. Part of our team she took the patrol car on to Palestine 100 miles away. Arrangements were made with Corsicana PD to pick me up each morning.

Saturday morning went off with out a hitch. The patrol unit was there to pick me up in five minutes. Sunday morning it was different. If I intended to eat at the camp I needed to arrive by 6:00 AM. The call was placed before that. Ten minutes passed, fifteen, twenty. I was going to be late.

Where was my police ride? Twenty five minutes, about to panic. I prayed Lord if they don't come soon, I'll miss my chance to go to the field. Missing the opportunity to meet and talk to people.

God always has a plan. As I opened the door to go call the police again, it opened. Out walked the top NASA representatives on site. We met briefly the day before when I told him, "I was sorry for his loss." We wanted to talk, but there had been no time.

He called me by name. "Dave I didn't know you were staying here. Need a lift?"

God's timing is always perfect. If the police had been on time I would have missed an opportunity to talk one on one with the man who had personally lost friends in the shuttle disaster. He had come to bring them home.

We talked on the way to camp, to share, and reflect, and get to know each other a bit. Sitting in the parking lot 10 minutes after we arrived still talking. He has a strong belief in God; his faith was seeing him through. He was a blessing to me.

Breakfast was eaten with plenty of time to spare. I decided to go to the van pool as workers loaded to go walk grids. Walking by each van as it was loading, giving the thumbs up sign and shouting to the crews to have a good day. Standing now at the front of the convoy, briefly saying a prayer as each van passed.

I left in the medical van with Ron a local paramedic, and Ann, a firefighter from Wyoming. During our 12 hour shift we were able to talk about EMS calls Ron had made and fires Ann had fought. Good venting.

Parking in the staging areas gave me a chance to talk to crew members on their breaks. My partners offered to take me to a grid closer to crews.

Leave it to God. We got stuck in the mud. Leave it to God. I got to walk through a grid to find help, seeing first hand what searchers were experiencing. Leave it to God. I got to walk and talk with those searching fields.

My final day in the camp beginning to say my goodbyes. Eating with the searchers, roaming through the command center taking to those I had gotten to know.

Watching a new load of workers arriving and being issued gear.
I saw fatigue on faces of those who would soon be demobilizing and sent home.

Beginning the drive back to our families I couldn't help but wonder if we had really been able to help. Do any good at all?

Then God reminded me, lessons learned at Ground Zero. Allowing people to ventilate and validate. But most of all we were just there, allowing people to experience "the ministry of His presence".

Am I Stressed Out?

Signs and Symptoms of Police Stress:

Headaches - Fatigue - Pounding Heart - Digestive Upsets
Teeth Grinding - Light Headedness - Lowered Sex Drive
Irritability - Short-tempered
Backaches - Muscle Aches - Over-eating - Insomnia
Restlessness - Muscle Tics - Rashes - Drinking too much

These are all common physical, behavioral and emotional reactions to prolonged stress. The stress that causes them may be obvious and acute as well as subtle and unrecognized. If you have just one and it disrupts your life or is upsetting to your family, you may be having a police stress reaction.

Prolonged stress, and I don't mean just having stressful situations occur fairly frequently, but I mean unrelenting and unresolved stress, sometimes bottled up over a period of years, can contribute to physical illness like cardiovascular disease and diabetes. Stress of this kind can also compromise the immune system and cause you to be more susceptible to everyday illnesses. Using alcohol even in moderation can mask underlying problems and lead to more serious problems in the long run.

Too many officers make the erroneous assumption that reacting to stress in their lives with emotions like anxiety and depression is a sign of weakness to be avoided, or at least hidden, at all cost. Thus warning signs are sometimes ignored. Incidents occur, you may feel upset briefly, other officers may joke about it, and you end up stuffing your feelings back inside.

As an officer dealing with other people's stress, your own denial can be so ingrained that you may not even experience stress emotionally. It may sneak up on you with physical symptoms or actual disease, or behaviors that put barriers between you and your loved ones.

Look at some of the stereotypes of officers in the media and how they are depicted dealing with stress.

The Captain swilling Maalox

The detective chain smoking

The stakeout car filled with fast food debris

The infamous donut everywhere

Having affairs

Contemplating "eating your gun"

And

The ultimate "cop bar" on my favorite show, Homicide

What's dangerous about these characterizations is that they all to some extent glamorize avoiding coping head on with the underlying causes of the stress.

The Most Common Causes of Officer Stress

Having treated several hundred officers I've reached the conclusion that ranked in order of prevalence, the most common causes are:

BOSSES

MARITAL CONFLICTS

OTHER FAMILY PROBLEMS

FINANCES

and lastly

What civilians may think of as POLICE STRESS, the actual stress?

Of The Job

The reason that the stress of the job is the least of the reasons that officers seek professional counseling is that what Joe Citizen may view as stressful in law enforcement work, officers accept and relish. After all, that's why you choose to have a career in law enforcement. I'm not minimizing the impact that dealing with a critical incident can have on you. Nor do I mean you shouldn't take seriously the insidious psychological effects of the build-up of cynicism and negativism that can come from dealing day in and day out with crime, criminals and the imperfect court system. I'm merely describing the frequency of presenting problems I see in my practice, demonstrating that more than anything else, law enforcement officers are human and subject in their own somewhat unique ways to the perils of being alive.

An Innovative Approach to Helping the Hurting: *The Associate Chaplain Program*

Although most Chaplains are well educated and have a wealth of training there are still needs in the lives of people we come in contact with we can't meet.

Our police department in Brownwood, Texas has three volunteer Chaplains and despite our education and training we still found there were situations where our skills were lacking.

Someone once said, "Great ideas are born from a need." So we began to think about what we could do to add the knowledge we needed to the Chaplain Program.

We targeted several areas, alcohol and drug abuse counseling and counseling with assessment. Both areas only provided by licensed persons. Each of us knew people in those fields of study who were Christians but their time was at a premium not to mention they didn't feel called to all the other areas of Chaplaincy.

From this, the concept of Associate Chaplains was born. We approached the city, the department, and those professionals with the idea of volunteering their time on an as needed basis. They were welcome to come work the streets with us if they chose, but what we really needed was their help in an "on call "capacity.

Everyone we approached liked the concept. So in late 2001 we added a Licensed Chemical Dependency Counselor to the Chaplain staff, and most recently a Licensed Professional Counselor.

The pair has strong Christian back grounds and the endorsement of their church and recommendation of their Pastor to serve as a Chaplain. They were given Police Department I.D. cards, and golf shirts with the wording Police Chaplain, on the back, and Associate Chaplain over the pocket. This would identify them as being with the department both to the officers and the public. The Associates work in street clothes and are not authorized to drive department vehicles or work alone. They are paired with a uniformed Chaplain that has additional advantages. On family disturbances and other matters it is nice to have a second Chaplain to work with one of the parties while you work with the other.

Our LCDC has little time to ride but responds when needed. On the other hand the LPC loves the streets and makes a point of working at least one shift a weekend with one of the regular Chaplains.

Most police Chaplain work is crisis intervention, so it is not uncommon to find someone in the mood to address their alcohol or drug problem, and the LCDC can actually start the recovery process by working with the person the same day and hooking them up with other local Resources and area recovery centers.

Our Chaplain LPC is handy at helping us make a determination on the scene of a crisis as to what the issues may be in dealing with a distraught or mentally ill person. This is particularly helpful in dealing with a "Barricaded Subject" or similar situation.

The adding of licensed personnel had brought additional credibility to the already successful Chaplain Program. The goal over the next year is to add a psychologist and possibly a medical doctor to the ranks of the Associate Chaplains.

Brownwood Police Department, Police Chaplain Services

CONFIDENTIAL AGREEMENT

The information contained in this report is confidential and privileged. If you are not the addressee, please be notified that any review or distribution is prohibited.

I______________________, have either been referred to/ or contacted on my own the Brownwood Police Department Police Chaplain Services.

I understand these services are confidential in nature, with the noted exemptions below:

(1) Chaplain will report to the head of my department and/or the director of human resources for the City of Brownwood that I have kept my scheduled appointments and may supply brief progress notes related to the counseling/consultation services provided. However the content of my conversations is protected.

(2) The Chaplain has an ethical responsibility to report if I am a threat to others or myself.

I understand if I terminate services that I may have been ordered to participate in; the Chaplain will report this action to my department head.

If I am referred by the Chaplain to a state licensed professional, the Chaplain may report that information to my department head and/or the director of human resources for the City of Brownwood.

I understand if I receive services rendered by the Brownwood Police Chaplains related to alcohol and/or drug abuse, such services are provided under Chapter 145 of the regulations and laws of The Texas Commission on Alcohol and Drug Abuse, based on an exemption for faith-based services.

Faith based providers operating under the 145 exemption must make the following statement:

The treatment and recovery services of Brownwood Police Chaplains are exclusively religious in nature and are not subject to licensure or regulation by the Texas Commission on Alcohol and Drug Abuse. This program offers only non-medical treatment and recovery methods, such as prayer, moral guidance, spiritual counseling, and scriptural study.

I have read the above statement and agree with its contents:

Client ________________________________ Date: ______

CHAPLAIN PARTICIPATION IN DEBRIEFINGS IS NOW OFFICIAL

The International Critical Incident Stress Foundation (ICISF) has officially said what we have known all along. Chaplains are a great asset in debriefings and defusings. Not only have they endorsed the participation of Chaplains, their latest 3rd addition manual on CISM has a section on chaplains and spiritual issues.

It is interesting this secular group was the one to come up with the adverse spiritual reactions resulting from a critical incident. One must wonder if we as Chaplains have been asleep at the wheel when it comes to being proactive in the integration of spiritual issues in previously secular programs.

Just as hospitals and the Joint Commission have long recognized Chaplains in the health care setting other groups such as the ICISF are opening doors for us. It is imperative we walk through them.

A Chaplain can not afford to believe college or seminary, or even CPE has prepared him or her to participate in debriefings or defusings. Like any other specialty CISM has specific training and exercises preparing you for this type of work. To be sure our training and experience in Ministry is a great asset. But we must avail ourselves of other excellent training available.

There are several debriefing models. The most recognized model is ICISF's Mitchell Model introduced by the organizations founder Jeff Mitchell. This model is especially useful in with the EMS population. There are other models such as the National Organization of Victims Assistance (NOVA) leaning to the civilian population.

While the Mitchell Model is appropriate for almost all settings, some in law enforcement, such as the FBI, has modified the format to better fit COPS.

Regardless of the model your department ultimately uses it is strongly recommended Chaplains go through at least the Basic Mitchell Model training. The Peer and Advanced training are also recommended.

As Chaplains we should use the ICISF formal inclusion of Chaplains as a wake up call to begin to explore other areas where Chaplains can provide valuable contributions.

CHAPLAIN COMPLETES STUDIES OF ISLAM RELIGION

Chaplain Dave Fair of Brownwood (TX) has completed the National Islamic Chaplain Training College. He has received his certification as in Islamic Chaplaincy, and is one of the few Christian Chaplains in the nation to become certified by the Muslim's own organization to minister to those of the Islamic faith.

According to Fair he took the training to better understand how to meet the needs of Muslims in a crisis through law enforcement or hospital Chaplaincy. The National Islamic Chaplain College made arrangements for Fair to take the training via audio and video tapes made during the on site training in Oregon, through a scholarship awarded to him.

According to Fair, after 911 many Americans became afraid of Muslims. "What really happens are people become afraid, and often the media builds a hybrid religion surrounding those fears? In the case of Islam the issues became violence, treatment of women, and conversion by the sword." Fair noted.

"These were the core fears of most people and while these issues may not be true, especially for all Muslims, they are what are discussed most by non Muslims. As a result it is what people fear, and they believe the Islamic religion and all Muslims are that way." he concluded.

Fair says as Chaplains we must be ready and willing to minister to people of any faith or no faith.

Fair is a Certified Master Chaplain with the International Conference of Police Chaplains. He is also a member of the National Association of Jewish Chaplains.

New Debriefing Models Can be Quickly Learned by Peer Supporters

Several new procedures have hit the streets to help Chaplains and their officers better deal with the effects of emotional trauma.

Once such program is Acute Traumatic Stress Management (ATSM), developed by Mark D. Lerner, PhD., and Raymond D. Shelton, PhD. The process addresses the emergent psychological needs of persons during traumatic events.

What's new about ATSM is it teaches emergency responders how to begin helping individuals as the event unfolds. This allows Chaplains and officers to start victims on the road to healing before the smoke clears.

Actually ATSM combines assessment of medical and physiological needs and gives steps for the worker to implement to help. While there are 10 stages to the process, the meat of the program is the Three D's. (1) Distraction, (2) Disruption, and (3) Diffusion. An emergency worker can begin these steps while treating a victim, or interviewing a witness.

To learn more about ATSM order the book Acute Traumatic Stress Management from the American Academy of Experts in Traumatic Stress (631) 543-2217. The book is $19.95 plus shipping.

Another advancement in dealing with trauma is Narrative Therapy. It's a narrative approach to critical and sub-critical incidents. The new twist here is the understanding that incidents of less magnitude may need to be dealt with. Called sub-critical incidents the process is implemented when the very nature of an event impacts an officer due to his individual history and baggage.

The narrative Therapy is introduced on-line in a dissertation by Joel Fay. An abstract review all current debriefing models then sets about teaching officers and others how to conduct the process. The procedure called Sub-Critical Incident Stress Debriefing (SCISD) is a hybrid of Brenner and Quinn's ABC Model, and the Everly Safe-R Model.

In brief the SCISD allows the officer to tell his story from beginning to end with out interruption. It then covers what the incident caused the officer to believe about himself (a mutual understanding of the event). The process then explores the origin of the belief and overlays a time the officer thought well about himself. In closing the officer is helped to find an alternative possibility to the story.

Information on SCISD can be found at www.narrativeapproaches.com/narativepolicing.htm.

The real beauty of these two rather new approaches is they are designed to be used with individual one on one. Although they require training and an understanding of traumatic stress they need not be conducted by a mental heath professional as is the case with CISD (Mitchell Model).

After reviewing the literature and applying the principals it seems the law enforcement Chaplain can glean useful information from the two models and then decide if he should do more in-depth training. Neither procedure seems to conflict with religious beliefs of the officer or Chaplain.

As Chaplains we owe it to those we serve to become aquatinted with additional ways to offer help in time of need, while insuring to do no further harm.

BROWNWOOD POLICE CHAPLAINCY RECEIVES FIRST ACCREDIDATION

The Brownwood Police Department Chaplain Program has received the first accreditation given in Texas from the Joint Commission on Law Enforcement Chaplaincy Accreditation and Education (JCLECAE).

Two representatives from the JCLECAE program were in Brownwood for a weekend as a site visit for the Brownwood program now in its 16th year.

Dr. Don Gibson and his wife conducted the site visit according to Dave Fair, Director of Chaplain Services for the Brownwood Police Department.

Fair said the group looks at the overall Chaplain program in departments. Inspected are the certifications and training of Chaplains in the program, how the program is integrated into the police agency and the community, and the array of services provided by the Chaplaincy.

"We were extremely pleased with what we saw in Brownwood", said Dr. Gibson, "the Brownwood Police Chaplain program is one of the oldest and finest programs of it's kind in the State of Texas."

Fair said he was very proud of the department Chaplains, Dr. Dan Chapman, who is the Deputy Director of Chaplain Services, Cal Gray, and Leatha Warden. "These Chaplains have put in thousands of hours of volunteer service to the department and the citizens, "

Fair noted, "We want to thank Police Chief Virgil Cowin for his support along with City Manager Gary Butts, and the mayor and council for allowing us to serve."

Chaplain program accredited

Photo contributed

Dave Fair (left), Director of Chaplain Services for the Brownwood Police Department, pictured with Dr. Don Gibson, Chief Executive Officer of the Joint Commission on Law Enforcement Chaplaincy Accreditation and Education and Tina Gibson, JCLECAE secretary. The two JCLECAE representatives inspected the Brownwood chaplaincy program and awarded the program the first accreditation given in Texas by the JCLECAE.

February 18, 2004 / Brownwood Bulletin / Page 5A

In a recent report to the Brownwood City Council it was noted the Chaplains over their 15-year service have donated over a $ 1,000,000 in time to the department and the community. The council was also given these statistics from the Chaplain program, over the 15 years:

- 131,000 volunteer hours for $1,314,000 in donated time.
- Patrolled 273,750 miles
- Worked 1,560 attempted suicides
- Attended 2,340 death scenes
- Did 360 death notifications
- Provided Chaplain services to 10,950 people

The local Chaplains over the years have been involved in various ways with the following major events:

- Total of three weeks in New York after 911.
- Spent a week in Killeen following the Luby's massacre there.
- Were on call in the Waco Branch Davidian incident.
- Debriefed the Chaplains from the Oklahoma City Bombing
- Served in east Texas during the Columbia Space Shuttle disaster recovery.

"We have served under three Chiefs", says Dr. Dan Chapman, "Joe Don Taylor who started the program, Joe Robbins, and currently Chief Virgil Cowin. We owe the success of the program to the Chief, officers, and civilian employees ", he said.

The Police Chaplains deliver death notifications, offer comfort at death scenes, and offer help in family violence, sexual assault and child abuse cases, to victims, and their families. The Chaplains are also involved in suicide intervention and prevention, crisis negotiations, and a host of other services, including counseling to the department employees and their families.

The Brownwood Program has expanded to offer services to almost every law enforcement agency in the county when needed The most recent addition to the Chaplain's duties is serving as a First Responder for the MHMR Crisis Team after hours, on weekends and holidays, for mental health emergencies. The Chaplains also serve the Brownwood Fire Department.

The Chaplains maintain an office at the Brownwood/Brown County Law Enforcement Center. They also respond in a fully equipped Chaplain vehicle.

The Chaplains have received hundreds of hours of training. Two of the Chaplains hold doctorates, one is working on a PhD and the other has a master's degree. In addition Chaplains are certified by The International Conference of Police Chaplains, of which Chapman is a state director."

The Chaplains maintain a web site on the City Of Brownwood's Web Pages, and provides a speakers bureau. For more information contact the Chaplains through the Police Department.

Clinical Pastoral Care in Law Enforcement Chaplaincy

Training Is Easier Than You Think

When I first became a Chaplain, I must admit I thought Clinical Pastoral Care was what a Pastor did. Little did I know there is a big difference in Bible college training and Clinical Pastoral Education. CPE got its wings in the health care industry. It didn't take Chaplains long to figure out there is more to Chaplaining a institution than looking at it as a Pastor and congregation. The analogy is there, but that's were it ends.

CPE is professional training for ministry. It integrates into pastoral work, theology, psychology, sociology, and ethics, and in the heath care setting medicine. It gives Clergy hands on encounters with real people. Thus allowing Ministers to develop their interpersonal relationships, leadership, pastoral care, and counseling.

Pastors when tending their flock are expected to preach the denominational line and to operate their parish by a set of guidelines, usually established by an ecclesiastical body. Counseling and related activities take on the flavor of the denomination.

Dealing with one's flock in the church setting is much different that dealing with people encountered in the Chaplaincy of health care, or law enforcement. Unfortunately ministers new to the Chaplain's role may find out too late about the differences. It is of the utmost importance we instruct new Chaplains in the principals of Clinical Pastoral Education.

Before we say the job is too great, and that it takes years to learn the ropes, we need to look at what The Baptist General Convention of Texas has done. In a course for volunteer heath care Chaplains, they have developed 42 hours of instruction. This includes 30 hours of basic pastoral ministry training and 12 hours of contextual training in a specific field of ministry. A certificate is issued upon completion of class room training. In addition there is 6 months of field training.

Having been through the classes twice over 5 years I came away believing we are missing a lot of important areas in our Law Enforcement Chaplain training.

When was the last time non Catholic Chaplains learned the context in which they can administer last rites. When is the last time we learned from a Muslim or Hindu about their faith so we could minister to those of like faith?

In law enforcement Chaplaincy we must understand we have a Spiritual mandate with secular accountability. In addition to the so called " social work " activities of Chaplains there is a real need for us to understand more about other religions, about ethical considerations, and areas of CPE we may not know or understand.

One way the Brownwood Police Department Chaplain Program in Brownwood, Texas handles the task is through Chaplain Interns. Once a minister is admitted to the program and has completed initial basic training, they become an Intern and must work under the supervision of a Chaplain for a year. Only then are they granted full Chaplain status, and are allowed to wear the uniform and respond alone to curtain type calls.

During the Internship the Chaplain Intern is monitored and instructed in areas of work not taught in class. It is strongly urged that new Chaplains complete the Baptist General Convention of Texas Volunteer Chaplain or similar training.

The training is not Baptist specific and non Baptist Chaplains can supervise field work. The regular Police Chaplain acts as Field Supervisor and signs off on the practicum form. At that point the BCGT issues a seal for the original certificate certifying the Chaplain as an approved Volunteer Chaplain.

Although the BGCT course is primarily aimed at health care, it does offer a criminal justice field training period and a CJ Chaplain manual is in the draft stage. Any Chaplain new or old can benefit from this course costing no more that $50.00, taught locally, usually on week ends and compliable in 6 weeks.

The BGCT Volunteer Chaplain training is one quick and inexpensive way to familiarize Chaplains with Clinical Pastoral Education and Care, and make them more cognitive of areas of Chaplaincy greatly differing from their role in a church setting.

I'm not saying a 42 hour course offers a full Clinical Pastoral Education, but there is enough in its content to cause a Chaplain, to "do no further harm"

I'm sure there are other similar programs in other denominations. We as Chaplains currently in programs should avail our selves of what is available.

When a new Chaplain couples ICPC Basic Certification with something like the BGCT program they will have the basics needed to do a good job. Then if you add an internship program you will find within a six months to a year the new Chaplain should be well suited for any assignment.

Dave Fair's Ground Zero Diary

Speech Delivered Patriot's Day

(1) Opening comments:

It was a great honor to be chosen to respond to New York last year following the 911 World Trade Center collapse.

I went as a Police Chaplain attached to the New Jersey Critical Incident Stress Management Team, assigned to the Port Authority who operated the World Trade Center.

A Stress Management Team helps emergency workers such as police, fire, and EMS deal with their emotional response so they don't burn out or have a nervous breakdown.

While in New York I worked at ground zero, at Belleview Hospital and morgue, and assisted in the command center.

I talked to dozens of emergency workers, visited with surviving family members, and visited some of those hospitalized after being pulled from the collapsed towers.

At ground zero we were required to wear the same dress as the rescue workers, hard hats, gloves, and masks to filter out the dust and smoke. It was still burning at 1600 - 2000 degrees.

My first day at ground zero was actually night. The scene was lit with portable stadium lights giving it the look of day.

It was all so surrealistic. I stood there not fully believing I was actually there. If anyone had told me a month before I would be standing where the World Trade Center once stood I would have said they were crazy.

There was just so much devastation, pilled 5 or six stories high. It looked like the world's largest trash heap.

There were two kinds of work going on. First there was the rescue effort. Firemen and policemen digging by hand to try to find survivors or recover bodies.

The second effort was large construction equipment moving the huge steel beams and other debris. There were curtain areas given specific names. There was “the pile “where the debris was heaped together, then there was “the pit", where workers were digging by hand. Ground Zero became known as Ground Hero in honor of those who lost their lives saving people.

As sad and devastating as the loss of over 3,000 lives was, we must remember there were some 50,000 people in the twin towers. That means over 45,000 people made it to safety.

Police, fire, and EMS workers risked and many lost their lives guiding these survivors to safety. Some actually carried or drug them out.

Of the dead, over 300 were New York City Firemen, and over 50 were New York and Port Authority Police Officers. The FBI lost one agent, and as a side note, that agent who had just retired from the FBI, had started work for the Port Authority two weeks before and was killed in the collapse. A friend told me, if he hadn't retired, he would have been heading the federal investigation.

Less than a week after the tragedy no more survivors were found. However rescue workers hoped against hope they would still find someone alive.

Firefighters have a saying, “No one goes home until the last man goes home “referring to their fallen brothers. So they continued to dig by hand until they were forced to stop and the operation was ended.

Sadly many bodies will not be found hampering closure for many friends and family. The heat has incinerated many of the bodies.

Some police officers were identified only by the serial number on the gun.

The City of New York massed together tremendous resources. An entire school gym was filled with rescue supplies, rain gear, lights, and everything else that was needed by rescue workers.

Food was never in short supply. Because the Port Authority operates LaGuardia, JFK and the Newark airports they contract with Marriott for food service, so food was delivered to a number of places for rescue workers and support staff.

Because there was fear of contamination there were hundreds of portable hand wash stations. There were even places where they washed your boots before you left the area. There were hundreds of portable potties to meet the needs of workers.

The Red Cross brought in a three deck cruise ship and docked it near Ground Zero. Two decks were to feed us. The third deck has cots to rest on and volunteer chiropractors and massage therapist helping get workers back in the recovery effort.

The attitudes of the workers, and even the survivors were much better than I expected. They seemed to have a purpose. If they could recover bodies they would be content. Each time a body or even body parts were found there was a since of relief. If the body was a fireman or policeman a color guard accompanied it to the temporary morgue.

I went there to help them, but they helped me to come back with their high spirits and gratitude. I expected to come back devastated but instead came back blessed. God keeping me above the cloud of despair.

Rescue workers were working 12 on and 12 off 7 days a week to start and then reduced to 6 days a week. The Chaplains worked the same schedules.

There was a make shift canteen at Ground Zero where food was served. And each night some celebrity would come to help serve. I met Brook Shields, and there was also some Pro Wrestlers, Mayor, and Senator Hillary Clinton.

Everyone had a story. At Belleview Hospital, there was an area called the “Blue Wall", during construction earlier in the month workers put up a plywood fence and painted it blue. Survivors now put up pictures of their missing friends and relatives in hopes someone would find them among the injured or recovered. A make shift memorial was started along the wall with flowers and candles.

Other memorials were at Fire Station 10 across from the WTC that lost 14 men and at the Port Authority HQ, as well as the police and fire existing memorials near the river.

There were stories of those who survived the 1993 bombing only to perish in this attack. Others survived both terrorist acts.

Every cloud has a “Silver Lining ", to me there are 4 very positive things that came out of the 911 tragedy.

- Patriotism- this is still seen nationwide. Every where you go even today, there are flags and plenty of red, white, and blue on tee shirts, caps, and bumper stickers. And of course now 911 being called Patriots day.

- People came together in time of need. I saw rescue teams from Mexico, Colorado, California, Illinois, Texas and many more. The officer I visited in the hospital, though in great pain, told me to thank everyone who came. He couldn't believe how much help there was.

On Sept. 10th people on the streets of New York wouldn't even make eye contact. But after the attack, as I was walking in downtown New York City, I saw a man drop something on the sidewalk and people stopped and helped him look for it.

- There is also increased awareness of God, in a positive way. Not where God, but rather God was was was there, with us.

Because I work as a Chaplain around so much death and trauma, let me give you my insight as to why “Bad Things Happen To Good People”. I don't believe tragedy is caused by God.

There are in fact laws that are in effect.

First is the law of gravity. A wheel comes off a car, it is apt to wreck. A wing breaks off a plane, it will crash.

The second law is, " Mans Free Will ', we are free will moral agents. Man makes bad choices and suffers the consequences.
God will not over ride a man's free will.

In the Garden of Eden, God told Adam and Eve not to eat the apple, the fruit of the forbidden tree. Yet they did any way. God didn't stop them. He allowed them to make a choice, even a bad choice, and to suffer the consequences. Banished from the Garden.

In the Old Testament God says, I set before you today, life and death, blessings and cursing. I want you to choose life. But God says you must choose. Man chooses and God lets him live with even the bad choices, although it breaks His heart.

- The final positive thing I saw was a renewed respect for Law Enforcement. Even crime in New York was down, it affected even the criminals.

I want to begin to wrap up on this note... one night I was standing on the deck of the Red Cross Ship. I had been at Ground Zero. I was hot and tired. Behind me I could see the lights at Ground Zero. But as I looked across the water I saw another light, another site. I saw the Statue of Liberty standing tall in the harbor, and it was if God was saying to me " Dave It's gonna be alright".....and I fully believe it will.

Here we are at 911 '02 Patriots Day. We live in the greatest country on earth.

We have a choice to be either victims or survivors. It's time now a year later to be survivors. We need to keep on praying, keep on loving and keep on being faithful in what we know to do that is right.

God is with us in the storms of life, the Bible tells us that He will never leave or forsake us. Thank you and may God Bless You and Yours.

Mental Health Chaplain Protocol

POLICE CHAPLAIN 1st RESPONSE
FOR MHMR MENTAL HEALTH CRISIS

GOAL: To help facilitate Crisis Resolution in the field, by first responding, to mental health emergencies. To return officers, to patrol as quickly as possible, to expedite the proper intervention of crisis for local citizens, utilizing resources including CTMHMR.

Limitations: Chaplains are at all times to work within their personal scope of training. Normally this will involve crisis intervention/ resolution, and pastoral care and counseling. Chaplains are prohibited from offering psychotherapy or similar clinical interventions unless they are trained and licensed.

1.1 Response: -

When the Chaplain is notified that their services are needed in a mental health emergency, the Chaplain will proceed to the location as quickly and safely as possible.

Unless the Chaplain is already in uniform when the response is requested the Chaplain shall dress subdued, keeping in mind some mentally ill persons are stressed by uniforms.
by stress. This mean lights and sirens, uniforms, shiny handcuffs and bright badges can have a negative effect on a person in crisis.

1.2 Assessment-

On arrival the Chaplain will speak with the officers on the scene as well as friends or relatives of the person in crisis. The Chaplain shall gather as much information available as quickly and accurately as possible about the person in crisis and the precipitating event or incident that triggered the situation.

These are several levels of assessment that can be done on the Chaplains arrival. The ***main question*** is always is the client **<u>a threat to self or others?</u>**

Use of the MHMR Suicide Assessment Sheet.

If it is evident the client is an immediate threat to himself or herself such as a suicide risk, then ***every precaution*** must be made to protect the client

The following options are available:

(1) Ask the client to voluntarily allow you to take them to the ER.

(2) Ask a law enforcement officer to make a warrant less Emergency Detention, of the person and transport them to ER.

(3) If time allows, execute the proper paper work and apply to have the client detained under a mental health warrant signed by a Justice of the Peace. When the warrant has issued any police officer may serve the warrant and transport the client to the ER.

Item #3 will require the assistance of the on call Crisis Worker.

If the person is not a threat to self or others at that time the Chaplain arrives the Chaplain is to attempt to defuse the situation utilizing standard crisis intervention skills.

In the event the Chaplain helps the person to reach a successful conclusion of the matter and the crisis is defused, the Chaplain may suggest the person be watched over night by a friend or relative

Another option is to have the person admitted to Respite. This is done when the person does not meet state hospital admission guidelines, and there is no family or friends to take the person home. Respite admission requires the involvement of the Crisis Worker.

If there has been any discussion or indication of suicide have the person sign a no harm agreement.

3.1. Transport to ER.

The local ER must medically clear all people in mental health crisis.

There are several ways to transport the person to ER.

(1) Family or friend of person, if stable

(2) Gold Star EMS, if not stable

(3) Police Officer, only on warrant less detention or mental health warrant.

(4) Chaplain, only if voluntary or on the request of the officer.

4.1 Options for the patient.

(1) Send home with family or friend

(2) Admitted to BRMC for 23 hour observation

(3) Sent to Respite

(4) Sent to state hospital

(5) Sent to private facility

All options must be made with the input of the MHMR caseworker and ERP.

5.1 Documents-

Chaplain at minimum will FAX the field contact document to MHMR. If other forms are used those should be given to the proper persons.

Brownwood Police Chaplain Program

The Brownwood Police Chaplain program began in 1988 in the old police station on West Commerce. Today, the Chaplains are part of the new Law Enforcement Center at 1050 West Commerce in Brownwood with an office across from Chief Virgil Cowin.

The Chaplains comprise a uniform division of the police department and serve in the field with the officers. Most Brownwood Chaplains are all members of the International Conference of Police Chaplains and are certified by that organization. They have received specialized training in suicide intervention, stress management, child abuse prevention, rape and crisis counseling, and a host of other related areas.

The Chaplains are available to department employees and their family members. In addition Chaplains assist victims, and witness's.

Some Chaplains are trained in Hostage / Crisis Negotiation and Critical Incident Stress Management. They are on call 24 hours a day 7 days a week to assist the officers when so requested.

The Chaplain program was expanded in the early 1990's to include the Brownwood Fire Department, where similar services are offered firemen and their families. Although the Chaplains are primarily assigned to the two public safety departments they respond to any city crisis involving city employees at the request of city staff.

Chaplains continue to receive in - service training both through the local department and through associations and other means. Recent training include the Columbine Tragedy, Lessons Learned, at Texas A & M, and Sixth World Congress of the Critical Incident Stress Foundation in Baltimore Maryland.

In the beginning there was no funding for the Chaplains and all expenses were paid by the individual Chaplains out of their own pockets. In more recent years funding for training has been

provided in the annual budget of the city, with assistance from some local churches, The Brownwood Municipal Police Association and individuals in the community. Chaplains donate 100% of their time.

Since it's beginning, Chaplain's have patrolled over 100,000 miles, worked more than 150,000 man hours donating more than one million dollars in time to the city.

Currently serving as Chaplains for the departments are Dan Chapman, Cal Gray, Bob Riley and Dave Fair. Chapman and Fair hold Master Chaplain Certifications while Gray holds a Senior Chaplain Certification. All Chaplains are ordained Ministers. Chapman also served as the Texas State Representative for the International Association of Police Chaplains.

Various chaplains are assisting other departments. Chapman is Chaplain for the Early Police Department, while Fair serves as Chaplain of the Brown County Sheriff's Department. Chapman and Fair also both serve as Chaplains for the Texas Department of Public Safety Critical Incident Response Team.

(From City of Brownwood (TX) Web-site)

Good Sam Crisis Intervention Model

Based On Luke 10:30-37

Luke 10:30-37

31 A priest happened to be going down the same road, and when he saw the man, he passed by on the other side. 32 So too, a Levite, when he came to the place and saw him, passed by on the other side. 33 But a Samaritan, as he traveled, came where the man was; and when he saw him, he took pity on him. 34 He went to him and bandaged his wounds, pouring on oil and wine. Then he put the man on his own donkey, took him to an inn and took care of him. 35 The next day he took out two silver coins and gave them to the innkeeper. 'Look after him,' he said, 'and when I return, I will reimburse you for any extra expense you may have.' 36 "Which of these three do you think was a neighbor to the man who fell into the hands of robbers?" 37 The expert in the law replied, "The one who had mercy on him."
Jesus told him, "Go and do likewise."
(From New International Version)

(1) ***Took pity on him:***

- (a) ***Notice people in your surroundings***
- (b) ***Physically and emotionally reach out to those in crisis***

(2) ***Went to him:***

- (a) ***Go to people where they are, meet them where they are***
- (b) ***Make the effort to go, and get involved***

(3) ***Bandaged him:***

- (a) ***Get your hands dirty, get directly involved in the intervention***

(4) ***Poured oil and wine*:**

- (a) ***Bandage them physically, emotionally, and spiritually ministering to their needs right then, right now, including food and drink***

(5) ***Put him on his donkey*:**

(a) Don't leave him in the crisis, remove him from the crisis location or remove the crisis from him.

(6) Took him to an Inn:

(A) If they have no place else to go, provide shelter and rest for them, after the trauma.

(7) ***Paid for follow up care*:**

(a) ***Use your resources on behalf of the person***

(8) Got someone else to care for him.

(a) ***Connect them with someone to continue the help***

(9) When I return:

(a) Check back, follow up and refer if necessary

Every Day Heroes

Presentation to Groups on Dave Fairs Time at Ground Zero

I was privileged to be at Ground Zero, after 911 last year, working with police fire and EMS workers.

There were a lot of Hero's from 911.

Policemen and firemen who risked their lives to save some 40,000. Some of those hero's died in the collapse of the WTC twin towers.

Hero's like Todd Beamer who along with other passengers gave their lives to purposely crash a plane into a field in Pennsylvania rather than have it crash into the capitol.

These men and women were just like us. They lived their lives, they had good days and bad days, but when the chips were down, when the going gets tough something from deep within rises up and they go that extra mile and they become heroes.

Hero's aren't born; heroism isn't something that is taught.

The Webster's dictionary defines a hero as someone that is brave, someone with courage, and again these things are not taught.

They are developed in the trials and tribulations of life and they are hidden away in our heart for safe keeping until they are needed.

You have heard it said. Someone has Heart. That's what we are talking about. It is having heart, that makes heroes.

Heart, come from facing the trials and tribulations of life and winning anyway. Heart comes from facing the undesirable and during it anyway. Heart comes from not quitting and never turning back. Heart comes from persevering in life.

Heart comes from not complaining about our lot in life but embracing it and making the most of it.

Heart comes from knowing God and living and loving as Jesus did.

In life when something tragic happens we can become either, bitter or better. We can become and stay victims or we can gut it up and learn from adversity and become survivors become future heroes

Do you have what it takes to be a hero, will you be ready to act when adversity comes.

You can be, all it takes is heart.

May God Bless You

Organizational Structure for Deployment In Man Made or Natural Disasters

CHAPLAIN/ MENTAL HEALTH/ PEER GROUPS

(1) Professional Agency and Provider Chaplains

Providing services in accordance with their agency or organizational directives for employees and those they serve.

These are stand alone groups except where indicated

Independent Agency Chaplains

Brownwood Police Dept.- Mental Health Certified *
Early Police Department
Brownwood Fire Department*
Gold Star EMS*
Brownwood Regional Medical Center*
Brown County Sheriff's Office
Brown County Water Improvement District Lake Patrol*
Local Members Texas DPS CIRT- Chaplains
Brownwood Regional Airport- Airport Chaplains *

* Seamless Services

(2) ***SMART TEAM-*** Spiritual/Mental Health, Assessment, Response, Transition Team- Under Direction of Police Chaplains- First 72 hour gate keeper

Providing services in triage areas for victims and family assistance centers

Members

Certified Crisis Clergy
Certified Crisis Mental Health Professionals

(3) Brownwood Crisis Trauma Team

Providing services, (CISM, CISD) for emergency service workers and responders

Secondary services to community at large involving trauma, grief and loss issues through group process

Self governed through the Texas Dept. of Health CISM Network, International Critical Incident Stress Foundation Network.

Team Members

CISM Trained Mental Health Professionals

CISM trained peers

CISM trained chaplains

SMART TEAM

Training for Community Clergy and

Mental Health Professionals

(Including Introduction to Critical Incident Stress Debriefing)

An 8 Hour Basic Certification Course
Sponsored By:

Chaplain Unit, Brownwood Police Department and
Chaplain Services, Brownwood Regional Medical Center

Introduction – 15 minutes

Clinical Concepts – 60 minutes

People of Any Faith or No Faith
You Don't Become a Buddhist to Minister to a Buddhist
Meet Them Where They Are, Diversity, Culture, Ritual

Traumatology – Physical, Psychological, Spiritual Effects

Critical Incident Stress Management/CISD

Intervention Strategies - PTSD

Lunch Break

Disaster Over View
Includes video on disaster reactions

VICTIMLOGY

What to Say and Not Say, What to Do and Not To Do

Burnout / Refer Out

Confidentiality / Ethics

Crisis Intervention

Grief Process

Responder Role

Summary Q. & A.

Certification Exam

DEALING WITH EMOTIONAL TRAUMA FOR ARMY MEDICS

Helping Others & Yourself Survive Emotionally After a Critical Incident

Course Objectives

Upon completion the student will be able to:

1. Define critical incident stress/ traumatic stress
2. Understand the Flight or Fight Syndrome and its effects on soldiers and the civilian population.
3. To apply Emotional First Aid techniques to help facilitate calming of a patient
4. How to manage their own stress and coach others on managing theirs
5. Introduction to Critical Incident Stress Management (CISM) and Critical Incident Stress Debriefing (CISD), and how to use the process successfully to restore persons to their pre-incident level of functioning

An 8 Hour Basis Course

Instructor: David J. Fair, D. Min, Certified Master Chaplain, Board Certified Expert in Traumatic Stress.

1. **Introduction** – 15 minutes

2. ***Stress Concepts*** – 45 minutes Fight, Flight or Freeze, What did you do in the war Daddy?
   Gunny Sacking and verbal emesis

3. **Critical Incident Psychology For Dummies** – 45 minutes Physical, Psychological, Spiritual Effects- Acute Stress Reactions/ Post Traumatic Stress Disorder **(PTSD)** Fireman Video.

4. ***Some Days The Tiger Wins***: 30 minutes, Critical Incident Stress Management/CISM

5. **Hip Pocket Diagnosis and Intervention Strategies** : 60 minutes – Emotional First Aid, Visual Imagery, The Power of Suggestion

6. **Disaster/ Critical Incident Over View** - 45 minutes
   Includes video on disaster reactions

7. **Burnout / Refer Out :** 15 minutes

8. **Confidentiality / Ethics**: 30 minutes

9. **Crisis Intervention** : 45 minutes

10. **Emotional First Aid: :** 45 minutes, What to Say And Not Say, What To Do And Not To Do

11. **Grief Process** : 30 minutes

12. **Responder Role :** 15 minutes

13. **Summary Q. & A.:** 10 minutes

14. **Exam**

COL. DAVID FAIR "NATIONAL COMMANDER"

Col. Dave Fair is the commander of the Law Enforcement division of Chaplain Fellowship Ministries. Col. Fair has been a Chaplain for the Brownwood (TX) Police Dept. since 1989, currently serving as Director of Chaplain Services.

Col. Fair holds a number of degrees including a Doctor of Ministry from Lake Charles Bible College in Lake Charles, La. Fair also holds a PhD in Religious Counseling. He is also a graduate of Tarleton State University Law Enforcement Academy, Stephenville, Texas, and The Jackson Center, in Brownwood, Texas.

Col. Fair, is certified as a Master Chaplain, Traumatologist, Trauma Specialist, Pastoral Counselor, Christian Marriage and Family Therapist, Thereupon Therapist (Faith Based), Bereavement Specialist, Anger Resolution Therapist, and is a Board Certified Expert in Traumatic Stress, Diplomat, and Listed in the National Registry of Experts in Traumatic Stress, American Academy of Experts in Traumatic Stress.

Dr. Fair also holds licenses as a Professional Pastoral Therapist- Diplomat, and Clinical Christian Therapist. In addition Fair is a Certified EMT, and is licensed by The Texas Commission on Law Enforcement Officer Standards and Education as a Texas Peace Officer, Instructor, Mental Health Peace Officer, and Investigative Hypnotist. He carries a Deputy Commission with the Brown County (TX) Sheriffs Department.

Col. Fair led the debriefing team in Killeen following the Luby's Massacre in the early 90's; he spent a week at Ground Zero as a chaplain following 911, and was in east Texas during the space shuttle disaster recovery. He helped debrief the debriefers following the Oklahoma City Bombing and was placed in an on call status during the Branch Davidian siege in Waco.

Col. Fair is an ordained Minister, Elder and Trustee at Abundant Life Church. He was elevated to the position of Bishop by St. Thomas-A-Becket Episcopal Synod and University, Canterbury, Kent, England,

Col. Fair is a member of the Brownwood City Council, and The Board of Trustees of Central Texas MHMR. In addition to serving as Chaplain for the BPD, he is Chaplain for The Brownwood (TX) Fire Department, Brown County (TX) Sheriff's Dept. Brownwood Regional Medical Center, and Gold Star EMS. Fair is also a Chaplain for the Texas Dept. Of Public Safety and serves on its Critical Incident Response Team.

Col. Fair, is Director of Crisis Response Chaplain Services, and serves as lead debriefer for The Brownwood Crisis Trauma Team, a member of The Texas Department of Health, Division of Emergency Preparedness, CISM State Network, and the International Critical Incident Stress Foundation CISM Network. In addition to being a public speaker Chaplain Fair is a published author in the field of Chaplainry and stress management. Fair, who is bi-vocational is General Manager of RMI in Brownwood.

Col. Fair is married to the former Karen McBride. The couple has three children and four grandchildren.

The SMART Team

Spiritual, Mental Health, Assessment, Response, Transition TEAM.

Pilot Program Provides Local Residents with Better Care in Crisis

It has been said tragedy brings out the best in people. But sometimes it brings out the worst. Following mass casualty incidents rescue workers mobilize along with the usual support personal. This includes the Salvation Army, Red Cross, NOVA, FEMA and the clergy.

Although most people who enter a disaster scene are well meaning, some are untrained. And in some cases people posing as clergy members attempt to get to the scene or talk to family members. Unfortunately there have been reporters, legal representatives, and souvenir seekers that come in contact with those traumatized, while posing as ministers or other volunteers.

Despite a few impostors there are usually a number of local clergy members who turn out in force to be of assistance. In some cases clergymen will drive hundreds of miles answering "the call."

Oklahoma City, The World Trade Center, and the Columbine shooting are just a few examples where it was difficult to contain the influx of clergy and mental health workers. Many "self dispatched "to the incident. Some causing more harm than good.

There were a number of horror stories where well-meaning ministers or counselors said inappropriate things to victims or family members thus adding to the trauma.

Brownwood has decided to protect its citizens from this type of thing in the event of a mass casualty incident or disaster. Worried about history repeating itself by way of secondary trauma, a group of police and fire and EMS Chaplains in Brownwood, developed a plan.

Included in the plan is training for local clergy, and mental health professionals, along with a security clearance system limiting contact with victims and families. Additionally the group set up a clearinghouse for outside mental health, CISM, or spiritual support. Any outside group wanting to provide spiritual or emotional support and care to citizens in the first 72 hours must go through the clearing house.

The first order of business was to become official. James Cook, Emergency Management Director for the City Of Brownwood, approved the concept.

Then the Chaplains set out obtaining approval from all area law enforcement, fire/rescue, EMS, and hospitals to accept only Certified Crisis Clergy, or Crisis Mental Health Workers to have contact with victims and family members.

The Chaplains reduced their ideas to writing, and that was the birth of the SMART TEAM .The acronym is for Spiritual, Mental Health, Assessment, Response, Transition Team. The name pretty much says it all. The team trains clergy and mental health professionals in disaster response. It then serves as a clearing house working to make sure only those persons carrying Crisis Clergy or Crisis Mental Health credentials are in triage areas or family centers.

Once someone has applied for the Team and approved, they under go specific training. When training is completed, and an exam passed they become an approved member. If they are called to the scene of a disaster they wear special identification tags. In addition they must also display a special "color of the day "tag worn with the I.D. The color of the tag changes daily to insure security.

According to Fair, "There are several groups who are pre approved. Naturally the American Red Cross will be involved, as they have the mandate from the National Transportation Board to provide Disaster Mental Health Services in transportation disasters. We have recently met with their local representatives to line out a local plan so things will go smoothly.

Anyone attempting to provide services to victims or family members in triage areas or family waiting areas without the appropriate identification will be removed from the scene.

So far according to Police Chaplain and SMART Team Director Dave Fair," We have trained and certified 18 clergy persons and 15 mental health professionals. "These volunteers will augment the existing police, fire, EMS, and hospital chaplains", Fair noted. " Those agency Chaplains will already have their hands full at the scene and victims in the triage areas such as the walking wounded and delayed transport will need comfort", he concluded.

In addition Fair says, "There will be a need to support family members who come to centers set up for them to find out about missing relatives."

According to Dr. Dan Chapman, Deputy Commander of the Police Chaplain Unit of the Brownwood Police Department, "Our goal is to make sure our citizens receive only the highest quality of care. We don't want untrained people having access to them, nor do we want too many trained people on the scene causing confusion."

Local officials admit the concept is unique but given the problems in past disaster situations they say the plan, complete with security clearance is perfect to protect citizens of the area.

The training for clergy and mental health professionals is basically the same. The clergy classes however, have a component covering Clinical Pastoral Education concepts. The remainder of the training covers introduction to CISM, disaster mental health and spiritual reactions. The do's and don't of working with family members, and a mock debriefing are also included.

There is wide use of videos exposing the participants to actual and reenacted disaster scenes. The videos cover a variety of issues clergy and mental health professionals are likely to encounter in the first 72 hours following an incident.

Says Chapman, "Our main concern is the first 72 hours after the incident. Following that other systems are usually in place to take care

of the long term needs of victims and families. "Chapman adds, "By that time there should be adequate support from local churches, family, and friends and outside support networks in place. Our goal is simply to restrict inappropriate emotional and spiritual exposure during the initial hours when our people are most variable.

According To Leatha Warden, who volunteers her time as the groups Clinical Director "We train the volunteers in "emotional first aid". It's too early in the crisis for formal counseling. It's a time for hand holding, giving emotional encouragement and support. For clergy, we call it the "the ministry of presents", she concluded.

Local SMART Team officials hope to be able to train those in other Texas communities in the concept as well as offer the local training again later this year. According to Fair, the San Antonio Police Department has requested information on Brownwood's SMART Team concept. Earlier this year Fair, presented the concept to the State Crisis Consortium in Austin.

Police Chaplain Do's And Don'ts
In The Medical Setting
Making Your Ministry More Effective

The Do's- With the Family

1. Be friendly but professional. Use Mr. or Mrs. unless told different.
2. Be aware of the children- does the family want them to hear
3. Make sure you are talking to the proper persons
4. Know the legal order of kinship. Spouse is before parent
5. Wear your name badge and dress appropriately
6. Offer water, coffee, wet rag, phone
7. On out of town calls the Chaplain will place through the operator
8. Do not touch or hug without permission
9. Be aware of any impairments ie: hearing, language barrier
10. Determine who spokes person is. Difference in cultures
11. Remember HIPPA applies, especially on the phone
12. Gather information from the nurse or doctor for the family if ok'ed by nurse
13. Be aware the nurse or social worker will ask about organ donation
14. Does the family want to see the body, if so prepare them?
15. Exhibit the "ministry of presence", don't talk a lot
16. Do listen. Ask open ended questions to encourage venting.

Don'ts – With the Family

1. Do not use platitudes like, God needed her in heaven, etc.
2. Don't give false hope
3. Do not pray out loud unless asked. Be aware of believe system. Ask!
4. Don't become caught between family members

5. Do not give advise unless asked
6. You cannot promote one funeral home. Must give names of all the locals
7. Don't give opinions on issues surrounding the incident or death
8. Don't ask a lot of questions.
9. Do not repeat anything you hear in the trauma room to the family
10. Do not repeat anything you hear from the EMS personnel
11. Do not criticize the hospital, EMS, docs, or others
12. Don't give information such as; he had been drinking, etc.

Don'ts in the ER/ Trauma Room

1. Do not get in the way
2. Do not "hover" over or around the patient
3. Even if unconscious, watch what you say
4. Do not interrupt doctors or nurses when they are working
5. Never give patients information about others involved in the incident
6. Do not try to diagnose or give your opinion to staff or patient.

Do's In the ER/Trauma Room

1. Encourage the staff
2. Grieve with them
3. Ask open ended questions during grief to allow to vent
4. Ask staff if they need something to drink
5. Ask if they need any help
6. If conscience encourage the patient but don't comment on condition
7. Adult patients have a right to have no one but staff with them
8. Ask if you can notify someone or their pastor
9. Ask if they want a family member with them, if permitted
10. Remember HIPPA applies

Chaplains Fair, and Warden operate both a Crisis Intervention Program, as well as a Private Practice. Warden holds a Masters Degree and is a Licensed Professional Counselor. Fair holds a Doctor of Divinity, and is Board Certified as an Expert in Traumatic Stress. He is also a Certified Christian Marriage and Family Therapist.

Reinventing Yourself and Your Chaplaincy

The Real Make Over

A chaplain may find himself or herself in a situation where he/she feels ineffective. H/she may have taken over someone else's Chaplaincy program or be assigned the task of making changes within the program itself. Regardless of the assignment, there may be any number of reasons the Chaplain and/or the program is on shaky ground and in need of change.

When a person or program needs change, it is easy to become overwhelmed. This is especially true when stepping into a new position, and even more so when having to restructure a program someone else has developed. However, there is hope and help available. For example, by utilizing a retail sales business model, someone can literally reinvent themselves or their chaplaincy program.

Businesses can fail for any number of reasons. It may be a poor location. Perhaps there is an ongoing failure to carry products that are necessary for a particular region of sales. It might even be a customer satisfaction issue, such as a complaint that has not been dealt with effectively or to the customer's satisfaction. Individuals can fail in the business by taking too long on coffee or lunch breaks. They may just sit in the back of the store and not greet or serve customers. They could even have poor personal hygiene. Whatever the reason business success is affected.

If you are in a situation where you need to make changes, you can use these examples of "business killers" as a guide to reinvent yourself or the entire chaplaincy program in your department. Problems in the program or even with yourself must be given your undivided attention. The inappropriate behaviors or situations you tolerate will not change on their own and they will continue to have a negative effect until addressed.

Most of the time when change is needed a proactive approach (one where you choose to make the changes rather than be directed to) is more desirable and effective. Consider the following proactive approach of how the Brownwood Chaplaincy program obtained an office.

You have heard it said, in business the key to success is location, location, location. In the Brownwood (TX) chaplain program we only had a small desk out of the traffic flow. Today we have a full office right across the hall from the chief, computer and phone included.

The office was not obtained by reactive behavior. We had to lobby for the location. We wanted to be highly visible to the officers and staff. This let them know where we were, but more importantly that we were available to assist them with any needs that might arise. It is difficult to sell any product if it is hidden in a corner.

In Chaplaincy we must make sure we are carrying the right "products". In the early days, chaplains prayed at department events, conducted weddings and spoke at funerals. This was all most people knew about the program. Today the police chaplaincy addresses a much broader scope of needs. One of the needs the program addresses is serving much like an employee assistance program (EAP). Functioning in this capacity is saving the department thousands of dollars.

It is important; to be effective that we redefine what people need from the chaplaincy programs today. While chaplaincy programs may be old school, the ministry we offer must meet the demands of a new curriculum. There are several other ways Brownwood has attempted to meet the needs of our Police Force. For example:

- Two of our chaplains have been to FBI hostage negotiation training. They are now able to act as consultants, or even as back up negotiators.
- Another chaplain is an emergency medical technician (EMT). He is able to provide minor emergency care in the field to both officers and victims. This is especially important, because often a chaplain arrives before emergency medical personnel. This chaplain can already have a patient's vital signs and necessary basic information, thus saving the paramedic's critical time.

- All chaplains have been to traffic school. Each of them can assist with traffic control at accident scenes.
- All Chaplains have had CISM training, thus they conduct department debriefings.

The list could go on and all. You can call it "add on purchasing", or "value added services"; at any rate it can greatly enhance the programs visibility, reliability and desirability.

By way of customer complaints, if there is a complaint about a chaplain from an officer or the public, then it is dealt with the same day and put to rest. This alleviates tensions between everyone involved, keeps a smooth functioning program and reduces negative gossip that could undermine program effectiveness.

As a chaplain program we require our individual chaplains to be proactive, Chaplains are not just sit in the office but to go to briefings, ride with the officers, to be visible and most important to be available. Situations that chaplains are most likely going to be sought out to deal with happen out on the streets, not in the chaplain's office.

Personal hygiene speaks for itself. Chaplains are not working under cover, so don't dress or smell like it.

Marketing your "product" is important. Our program publishes a quarterly newsletter. It's not for birthdays and anniversary listings or comics. We use it to promote the chaplaincy. In each issue we highlight one or two of our "products". It may be a service one of the chaplains can now offer, having just came back from a school/training.

We talk about what the chaplain can now offer the department. It may be to announce that we are now carrying a jump kit in the chaplain vehicle for minor first aid, or a status board for hostage situations. In addition, we will provide information that can be of practical use to the troops. We may list the signs and symptoms of stress, or talk about grief reactions.

Another means that assists in making people aware of our program is through outreach to the public. This is accomplished by chaplains being represented in parades, civic clubs, and churches. We are always looking for opportunities to promote the ministry of the chaplaincy.

Involvement in civic activities helps us to know our customers as well. Knowledge about our customers is vitally important. We have made a list of our customers or possible customers and then we set out to increase our customer base.

It is a given the officers and civilian employees of the department are customers. We have met with the city manager and offered to do crisis intervention for all city employees.

We offer assistance to victims not just by our presents, but now we assist them with crime victim compensation forms. This is a new customer service. As a result of this, our chaplains have a developed a great relationship with the victim service workers.

Counseling can be a big part of chaplaincy as well. However, not knowing your limitations can cause you more trouble than you can imagine and even get you sued. Thus, our chaplains have identified thee types of counseling. The first is "tailgate counseling"; this is similar to peer counseling and does not require a license, although some training is helpful. The second is pastoral counseling; this is usually through an appointment in the office. Training in pastoral counseling is greatly preferred and more often than not necessary to be effective.

The third is professional counseling, and is done by or requires referral to a licensed person. Fortunately, one of our Chaplains is a licensed professional counselor. If someone in the department or a victim needs to be referred to counseling and has no insurance, this chaplain is able to see them through the chaplain's program at no cost.

Regardless of what your program offers, customer service by the chaplain and the program is the most important thing you can do. It requires meeting the expectations of our customers in three vital ways: Being dependable! Being professional! and Being Responsive!

Be Dependable: It is important that people who need a chaplain can depend on you for consistent services when they need it, and that you do it right every time. You must provide them with accurate information. It is better to take a little extra time to get the facts and services right that to go back and try to "fix" an error.

Be Professional: Always act professionally, to include dressing appropriately, being pleasant, friendly, and positive and as helpful as possible. One of the biggest traps is to get involved in department politics. Chaplains are there to help bring peace, not become a member of the political undertow of the agency.

Be Responsive: Be aware of the needs and respond to them. Be as helpful, accessible, and effective as possible. Be responsive to peoples needs in practical ways. We carry stuffed animals for children in crisis, water for victims and officers, etc. Also, we try hard to keep the back seat of the car clean. You never know when you might need to offer someone an opportunity to sit and rest under air-conditioning or heating.

As a chaplain you must always be ready to offer an alternative. To call the customer's pastor, to contact a therapist, to call someone who knows the answer to sticky questions, the priest, the rabbi.

One of our chaplains, recently finished, an Islamic chaplain certification course so that he could minister more effectively to individuals of that faith. Our chaplains have studied fact sheets on most all religions and thus, are now a resource for the community. Keep in mind; chaplaincy is about service not theology.

In the case of revamping a program, you must reinvent the chaplaincy, if it is not working. You must be bold yet patient. One suggestion is to make a big visible change to start. Changing the uniform colors is a good first step. It is a simple move, yet it shows a willingness to make modifications and changes. Have new radio unit numbers and badges assigned. Change things with high visibility so the officers and the community know that something new and good is happening. Then from the suggestions in this article continue to reinvent the program.

The same thing applies to chaplains who want to reinvent themselves. Changing the look signifies something is happening. If you have a beard or mustache, shave it. A special note here. Some departments have a policy about facial hair and length of hair. Some chaplains get those regulations waved for them, as they are usually volunteer. You need to understand if you are allowed to do something different than the officers are required to do; it breeds resentment and can hurt the program. When in Rome do as the Romans.

As individual chaplains we can start showing up at briefings. Even if the briefing is late at night, if you're there it will express your level of commitment to the officers. Ask to ride with that difficult officer, the one who has been resistant to the program.

It is usually never too late to reinvent and make change. Once in a while, however, for whatever reason, you have compromised yourself as a chaplain to such a degree that you are unable to repair the damage. If this is the case, resign with a good attitude while accepting responsibility for your actions.

Find an older chaplain from a different program that is willing to mentor you. Humbly allow them to help you work through what went wrong, how it could have been avoided and how to appropriately deal with similar situations before they get out of hand in the future. After you have utilized the retail sales business model to reinvent yourself, with the assistance of your mentor, start a new program for another nearby department. Remember wisdom is the better part of valor.

If you have just taken over a chaplain program that needs to be revamped, or you have started one from scratch, the ideas that have been presented will perhaps help you. But remember, your biggest asset in all you do as a chaplain is the “ministry of presence”. When you have done all you can do to stand, just stand.

Give your loving presence.

"THE SNICKERS MINISTERY"

Chaplain Leath's Warden's Story

She was really worried about the baby. Frail and having difficulty breathing the flights nurses had arrived.

Packaging the struggling infant to fly to the children's hospital, time was valuable.

The family didn't want to talk to a Chaplain, the word from social services and OB nurses. Associate Chaplain Leather Warden stood at the foot of the bed silently praying. Wondering about the baby's chances to survive.

Paramedic having trouble getting the tube, baby fighting, maybe that was a good sign. Nurse got the tube at last.

Dad in the corner of the room so stressed and worried. Leatha couldn't help but think, "If he would just talk about it". She takes a stab at general conversation. Little response.

Closer and closer to flight time, ready to roll the baby to the helo. New mom will be allowed to go on the one hour flight. Dad can not. Three to four hour drive. Will be hard, it's getting dark.

Dad nervous, worried about the baby, about mom, about the trip. Nodding to Leatha, "Yes it will be a long trip", looking away, silent now.

Maybe angry at God, who knows.

Loading the baby in the helo, loading mom. Nurse, paramedic and pilot ready to go. Dad saying a quick good bye. Standing with Leatha watching the bird fly away.

"He hasn't had supper", Leatha reminds herself, "wish I had something to give him." A bulge in her pocket. A candy bar. Her favorite a Snickers.

“Here take this, it’s not much but maybe it will help”. Dad accepts with a faint smile. A brief word of thanks. Dashing to the car he is off.

Leatha, on the sidewalk, wondering, prays. Thinking about the faint smile. The brief thanks. At last a connection.

“As you do to the least of these my breather you do to me”…Jesus. The Snickers Ministry has begun.

THE POWER OF LIFE AND DEATH IS IN THE TONGUE

Effects of the Placebo Effect

I'm Johnny Come Lately on the subject of faith and the placebo effect. I became interested in the subject after studying hypnosis, and thought field therapy. In researching the placebo effect and comparing its action to faith healing, there is a wealth of research already done on the subject.

The placebo effect is the measurable, observable, or felt improvement in health not attributable to treatment. This effect is believed by many people to be due to the placebo itself in some mysterious way. A placebo (Latin for "I shall please") is a medication or treatment believed by the administrator of the treatment to be inert or innocuous. Placebos may be sugar pills or starch pills. Even "fake" surgery and "fake" psychotherapy are considered placebos.
Yet it goes far beyond that.

The fact is the patient believed the sugar pill was medicine or the procedure was going to be successful. There is a Bible verse saying" For as he thinketh in his heart, so is he, "Prov 23:7 KJV. And that pretty much says it all. If we think something enough, the body actually begins to heal itself. The thoughts affect the immune process.

Some believe the placebo effect is psychological, due to a belief in the treatment or to a subjective feeling of improvement. Irving Kirsch, a psychologist at the University of Connecticut, believes that the effectiveness of Prozac and similar drugs may be attributed almost entirely to the placebo effect. This has all kinds of implications; it could explain why some tonic cured all of grandpa's ills. It could explain why Napoleon Hill's book, Think and Grow Rich" was so successful. It could even explain why some prescribed medications are highly successful.

Advertising agencies have long known about the power of suggestion. Drink a curtain beer and you get all the girls. Drive a curtain car and you become transformed into a different person. Verbal or visual it all impacts the brain, creating thoughts, feelings and emotions. Drug companies are becoming less inhibited about promoting their pills with actors on television. Simply by using words, planting suggestions, a physical body can be affected. For good or bad.

Stage hypnosis plays on the same idea. Some people are more susceptible than others. A savvy performer can weed them out promptly. The implications are staggering. The mind body connection is a proven fact. It has been clearly established that the brain is a major determinant of the activity of the immune system and the endocrine system. The interplay of the neurological, immunology, and endocrinology systems may also be a fruitful subject of research into the placebo effect.

Doctors in one study successfully eliminated warts by painting them with a brightly colored, inert dye and promising patients the warts would be gone when the color wore off. In a study of asthmatics, researchers found that they could produce dilation of the airways by simply telling people they were inhaling a bronchi dilator, even when they weren't.

Patients suffering pain after wisdom-tooth extraction got just as much relief from a fake application of ultrasound as from a real one, so long as both patient and therapist thought the machine was on. Fifty-two percent of the colitis patients treated with placebo in 11 different trials reported feeling better -- and 50 percent of the inflamed intestines actually looked better when assessed with a sigmoid scope "The Placebo Prescription" by Margaret Talbot, New York Times Magazine, January 9, 2001

Consider these hypotheses. A television faith healer stirs up "faith" in the crowd. Testimonies of those who have been healed are given. The crowd becomes more "excited". Around the parameter of the hall, are discarded wheel chairs, braces, and crutches. The speaker works to build "faith", asking, "Do you believe God will heal you?" How strong is your faith? The scene becomes more charged than a professional sporting event. The minister then "lays hands "on the person receiving prayer. Others loudly pray in unison. The person falls to the ground. Prayer continues. Ushers help the person to their feet, and then the person, apparently healed, sheds a brace and runs around the auditorium.

Does this happen? Sure it does. Did the minister do anything wrong or unethical? Probably not. If the preacher had told the person they could walk on hot coals they probably could. In human beings, there exists language that increases the possibilities of conditioning. For human beings words can function as stimuli, so real and effective, that they can mobilize us just like a concrete stimulus.

This scene could have been a real estate sales conference or a weight loss program. It's the old adage of "Mob mentality "Truth is the preacher did nothing really wrong. In the Gospels, Jesus asked people if they believed. While some may allege the preacher is a charlatan the truth is he appeared to be using the God given power of the human body to self heal. The trappings are all part of the "suggestion"

Fundamentalists are likely to take the position attributing any healings to the placebo effect is taking away from the power of God. However when one searches the scriptures a "positive attitude" was important in the healing process. It may have been called "faith" or "belief", but the end result was the same. One said, Lord I believe, help my unbelief, Mark 9:24.

To be sure all healing is not the placebo effect. In an experiment at the Mid American Heart Institute, Doctors wanted to make their experiment impervious to any placebo effects. They did not tell patients they were being prayed for — or even that they were part of any kind of experiment. For an entire year, about 1,000 heart patients admitted to the institute's critical care unit were secretly divided into two groups. Half were prayed for by a group of volunteers and the hospital's chaplain; the other half was not.

All the patients were followed for a year, and then their health was scored according to pre-set rules by a third party who did not know which patients had been prayed for and which had not. The results: The patients who were prayed for had 11 percent fewer heart attacks, strokes and life-threatening complications.

Yet the question persists, is it wrong to depend on the placebo and crediting it with healing? Does it distract from the power of God?

The Bible says all gifts come from God that He made and created all things. Every good and perfect gift is from above, coming down from the Father of the heavenly lights, who does not change like shifting shadows" James 1:17. If true then the placebo effect is God given, God made, and God inspired. Yet one should be careful in explaining the placebo effect. If not careful a person could come to believe God is not needed in the placebo process. This is where the Chaplain comes in. He or she can gently with the use of scripture explain that all good things ultimately stem from God.

The big question to wrestle with in this study is, "Does the placebo negate God, and is it simply all in the mind?" The question gets a little scary if you believe you have accounted for God's power being relegated to your own mind. Yet there is scripture that states God has equipped us with curtain abilities….equip you with everything good for doing his will, and may he work in us what is pleasing to him" Hebrews 13: 21"

The Bible says, the tongue has the power of life and death, Prov. 18:21 (from New International Version) Wow! You mean what we say can actually affect a person physically. You bet it can.

Having recently taught on this subject at church. I brought a spray bottle with me and in the middle of the teaching I picked up the bottle and sprayed it around in different directions. Asking the audience to raise their hands as soon as they detected a pine smell, several did. There was nothing in the bottle but water. A seed planted in their mind, a suggestion, and "as they believed in their heart, so they smelled".

At a recent men's breakfast, one of the guys told a story on the other. Remember when we used to tell Virgil how bad he looked. We would say he must be running a fever. Before the day was over Virgil said he felt feverish and went home sick. The story was true. Old Virgil was susceptible to suggestion, and he literally became sick, because people told him he was.

For all the good the placebo effect can do, there is a close cousin to it that's bad. It's the nocebo effect. And to be sure it is just as powerful but in a negative way. The nocebo effect activates from negative suggestions and speech. It's thinking in a way that will cause negative effects to the body and mind. Literally making you sick.

This is one reason medical doctors remove instruction and side effect sheets from drug samples. If you tell the patient they will get chills and fever as a side effect of a drug, you can be sure they will.

The word nocebo, Latin for "I will harm," doesn't represent a new idea -- just one that hasn't caught on widely among clinicians and scientists. More than four decades after researchers coined the term, only a few medical journal articles mention it. Outside the medical community, being "scared to death" or "worried sick" are expressions that have long been part of the popular lexicon, noted epidemiologist Robert Hahn from the Centers for Disease Control and Prevention in Atlanta.

A more deadly effect of the nocebo has been referred to as, "voodoo death". Some years ago I did a study of movements and cults. This included Afro Caribbean religions such as Santeria and the more dreaded black arts.

There were stories of hexes and curses and voodoo dolls. A story was related of a mistress wanting to harm her lover's wife. She placed a voodoo doll on the doorstep to be found by the woman. There were pins placed in the throat of the doll. The mistress called the woman on the phone; she could only answer but not talk. She was choking.

Can the nocebo effect be that strong? It appears it can. Witch doctors, medicine men and shamans perform spells or rituals. It seems if people believe the practitioner has the power to cast a spell then the spell (curse) works.

There have been several books written about what to say to patients in times of disaster or trauma. The most recent book, The Worst Is Over, goes chapter by chapter about building rapport with people injured or scared, and then to facilitate helpful recovery using voice and touch.

The words may be something like, "Most people I touch with two fingers on their forehead, seem to immediately feel their head ache leave and a cool breeze cover their body".

To make it even more powerful the practitioner may state to a child. "Will you be my partner and work with me toward making you feel better? Now when I touch your arm where it hurts, you are going to feel a gentle tingling meaning the arm has started to heal."

> This may be why alternative or complementary therapies are a multi billion dollar a year business. It can be magnets, Rieki, healing touch, acupuncture, and so many others that seem to work well. An unscrupulous person knowing the secret could make up almost anything he could do to a patient. If it was a good enough sell, it might work through the placebo effect. The unscientific healer does not need to observe the restraints of reputable medicine. Where true medical science is complex, the quack can oversimplify.

As a law enforcement officer studying hypnosis for memory recall of witnesses, it often worked with or without the relaxation technique, and trance induction. The power of visualization and suggestion worked as well. That's why some people are changing the name of what they do from hypnosis to guided imagery or progressive relaxation. Those are more acceptable words with less hocus-pocus involved.

We have established what appears to be a striking truth where thoughts and speech affect the human body. The truth can be used for good or for evil. Lt. Col. David Grossman (retired) speaks about why kids kill in a presentation he does for school administrators. Col. Grossman has a really good take on the correlation of what kids see and hear having an effect on them. Maybe it is possible a violent song played over and over can cause a boy to kill his parents. Evidence points to the power of suggestion being just that strong.

Experts who traced the Dungeon and Dragon games found the players stepped over the line from fantasy to reality when fed a steady diet of the mind games.

What do we as Chaplains do with all this? It is a lot to swallow in one sitting. There is no doubt this is one of the most powerful yet simple things that can be done to effect life and health. It is power. Real power. It is awesome to know you have the power of life or death in your tongue.

How do you articulate this to others? There are positive ways people use the placebo effect. Many do so without knowing it. By the same token people unknowingly use the nocebo effect too.

My uncle died of old age at 94. A doctor told Uncle Chick he had cancer of the bones when he was 75. Refusing to believe the doctor, he simply said, "I don't have cancer." He died some 20 years later. Never taking any treatment and not sick one day from the dreaded disease. But if the doctor had said you have only 3 months to live he would have probably been dead by then. A self-fulfilling prophecy.

Maybe doctors shouldn't give so much "bad news "to patients. That poses an ethical dilemma. But some of the old family doctors didn't tell their patients all the bad news. The doctor making a house call was often seen out of earshot of the patient talking to another family member about the prognosis. Not very long ago, the rituals and symbols of healing constituted the bulk of the physician's armamentarium. In the early decades of the 20th century, most of the medications that doctors carried in their black bags and kept in their office cabinets had little or no pharmacological activity against the maladies for which they were prescribed. Nevertheless, their use in the appropriate clinical context was no doubt frequently beneficial.

Is it possible to tell a patient less than is known about their condition? What about patient's rights? Would it ever be ethical to withhold information from a patient for the greater good?

Some doctors say it is a" crap shoot" anyway. There are so many factors. One can't say for sure how long a patient will live. So if we don't know, are we obliged to make a good guess? Why not say longevity depends on a number of factors, it involves what we eat, how we live, and what we think and say. Ultimately they are in charge of their own destiny. After all that's what patient's right are all about.

How can we as Chaplains use this information? How can we impart to others understanding of the power of the tongue. The power of "bad news" or a "good report"? Ethical dilemmas aside we can start to use the tools we have. Above all others we should be the “Good News” spreaders. Chaplains can model the placebo effect. At the same time we should point out to others when they are using the nocebo effect.

As we talk to doctors and nurses we can communicate the effectiveness of the placebo effect by actually speaking positive things into their lives. When they have a positive outcome we share with them what we have done.

What is the bottom line to the placebo effect? People talk about the upward spiral of health costs. There are tests, treatments, and procedures. Yet it could be, we have omitted the simple thing that mom and dad always knew. A few kind words and a kiss can make it all better.

One of the reasons for the wide and growing popularity of alternative medicine is its careful attention to those very aspects: Alternative practitioners typically give patients a thorough evaluation, listen to them, and pay attention to them--all in an atmosphere of high expectations for healing. That provides real benefit to patients, even if the particular therapy the practitioner is using has no intrinsic therapeutic effect.

Maybe each of us has the God given power to intervene in the health care crisis. All that’s needed is to simply speak positive, healing words into people’s lives.”

At that rate, a penny for your thoughts”, can become a really good deal.

References:

(1) , (2), The Placebo Effect- the Skeptics Dictionary- Robert Todd Carroll

(3) The Power of the Sugar Pill, Julio Rocha do Amaral, MD.

(4) Spontaneous Remission, and The Placebo affect, Stephen Barrett, MD.

Chaplain Dave Fair, (right), with longtime friend and colleague, Dr. Dan Chapman. Both Chaplains are FBI trained in crisis negotiations. The pair are shown during an International Conference of Police Chaplain's Conference in New Mexico. Fair is also a commissioned officer.

Chaplain Dave Fair, volunteered at Ground Zero working with the New York Port Authority. Bottom: Chaplain Fair shown with two members of the New York Police Dept. Taken at Bellview Hospital in NYC, After working the morgue, and visiting officers injured in the tower collapse. Top: Ground Zero

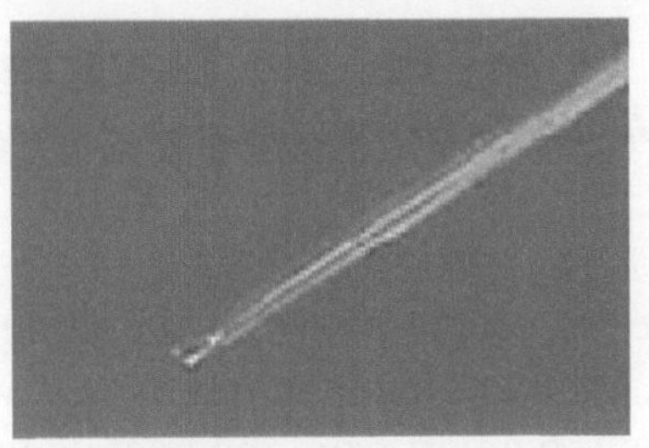

TO CLOSE TO HOME

Chaplain Dave Fair, was deployed to East Texas, to work with NASA, following the Space Shuttle Disaster (top). Debriefed a group of Debriefers, after the OKC Bombing. Did one on one work following the Branch Dividian Siege, Waco

If You Want To Be, Be. But Don't Be A 'Wanna Be'!

Dave's International Conference of Police Chaplain's Website Classic

A number of years ago while attending an ICPC training seminar, another chaplain and myself were sharing a ride-a-long in a unit from the host department. Several patrol cars, including ours, had become involved in a car chase. One of the lead units had stopped the fleeing vehicle. As soon as the unit in which we were riding got to the scene, but even before our car quit rolling, the other chaplain grabbed his flashlight and opened the car door. Immediately our driver said, "Hey. Wait a minute!"

I guess as chaplains we have all done that or at least thought about it, especially in the beginning of our chaplain careers. Make no mistake about it, many chaplains go through a "rookie phase" just like officers do. The real problem comes if the chaplain fails, after he learns the ropes, to make a clear distinction between the difference of being a cop and being a chaplain.

Certainly every chaplain has resolved, in his or her mind when the chips are down, a chaplain may have to take action and become involved in a situation when the officer needs assistance. But there should be clear roles that a chaplain is not to interfere with a call in any way unless so requested by the officer.

Most law enforcement chaplains have uniforms, badges and carry much of the same equipment as a regular officer. But some chaplains, who have not received formal police training and are not commissioned officers, step over the line into the officer's role. This is dangerous for the reputation of the chaplain because he can be tagged a "Wanna Be" by the officers.

This in no way says that a chaplain can not or should not participate in special roles for which he has been trained. Examples are family violence, crisis negotiation. Even traffic control or similar duties where an officer can be freed to tend to law enforcement business.

Should a chaplain desire to become a police officer, either regular or reserve, in that he can expand his usefulness that's fine. But the chaplain must pay his dues. This involves going to the police academy or some other approved means of training. Then the chaplain takes the state exam just like all other officers. Before a chaplain undertakes this course of action, he or she will want to discuss it with the Chief or Sheriff to make sure it meets with their approval.

What are the pros and cons of a chaplain also being a commissioned police officer? It depends on the agency, the policies, and the duties. Rough estimates say about 30% of chaplains carry commissions. Many just go through the academy for the experience with no thought of actually becoming an officer -- just wanting to learn what the officer actually goes through.

The bottom line is either be a chaplain or a chaplain/officer, not a "Wanna Be". Stay on the chaplain side of the fence or pay your dues, get the training, and earn the right. There can be no short cuts. "Wanna Be" chaplains create distrust among officers. They may question what is the chaplain more interested in, the streets or the ministry?

In closing, even a chaplain/officer must be careful. We are there always first as chaplain and as officers second. Use the fact that you are an officer to your advantage. You will know what officers really are going through and it can increase your chance for ministry.

Frankly, there is nothing wrong with wanting to be a chaplain only. It removes any doubt as to your motives.

DEFUSING ~ REFRAMING- INSTILLING HOPE

Learning To

DEFUSE ANGER~ INTERVIEN IN CRISIS ~ APPLY EMOTIONAL FIRST AID

In Foster Care

Presented by: David J. Fair, D. Min.
Director of Chaplain Services Hope for Tomorrow
(An adapted work)

BASIC CALMING TECHNIQUES

At the physiological level, calming a person who is frightened, anxious, or in a panic means shifting neurological activity from the *Sympathetic Nervous System* to the resting state *Parasympathetic*. Both systems are feedback loops in which senses, muscles, and brain are connected. If you control any part of the loop you influence the whole thing. That's the theory. Here's what to do on the ground:

RESTORE RHYTHM In calming, cadence is more important than content. Sympathetic activity is fast, jagged, and irregular. Give panicky people something repetitive and reassuring to focus on. Start loudly and rapidly enough to attract their attention then soften and slow. Go where they are, and gently lead them to where you want them to be. If all you do is repeat the phrase, *you're going to be okay* to the rhythm of an imaginary deep, slow drum, frightened people will eventually calm down.

FOCUS ON BREATHING Rapid, shallow panting works well for running or fighting, but merely fans the flames of fear when people are standing still. Hyperventilation causes all sorts of frightening sensations.

Have people take a deep breath, hold for 5 seconds while you count, then breathe out for 5 seconds. Slow, deep exhaling is the best cure for hyperventilation. *Do not* use a paper bag.

REWARD SMALL STEPS Give people an *okay* or *good* every time they do what you suggest. If you feel like a pre-school teacher, you're doing it correctly. If arousal increases – and it probably will – go back a step and bring them down again.

***GET* MOVING** Movement helps burn off excess adrenaline. A brisk walk is great. When that's not possible, have people tense, hold, and relax. Muscles that are involuntarily clenched relax more easily if they are purposely contracted first.

REDEFINE THE SITUATION The problem in panic is a malfunctioning alarm system. The fear is real but the danger it warns of is not. Frightened people think they are going to die, faint, wet their pants, or at least throw up. Don't get sidetracked by discussing the specific dangers they imagine, because as soon as you've talked them out of one, they'll think of another. Focus instead on the alarm system itself. Say: *You're having a panic attack. Your body is so full of adrenaline that it's hard to think straight, that's why you need to take the deep breaths to slow your mind down enough to start feeling better.* Then move back to the calming sequence. Obviously, if you have doubts as to the person's safety, call 911.

INTERRUPT ESCALATIONS People in the midst of an emotional explosion do not get better by getting things off their chest. Talking about how bad they feel only makes them feel worse. Don't be afraid to interrupt. It doesn't help to stand by politely letting people work themselves up when you're trying to calm them down.

Crisis Intervention Training- Hope for Tomorrow

Teaching Objectives

- A Definition
- A conceptual model
- Goal of Crisis Intervention
- Role of the Crisis Intervener
- Crisis Intervention Principles
- Crisis Assessment
- Crisis Action Strategies
- Steps of Crisis Intervention
- Crisis Intervention With Children: Don'ts and Dos
- More tips for counselors/chaplains/Parents
- Tips for parents
- Tips for Children
- Training Others

A Definition

Crisis is a perception of an event or situation as an intolerable difficulty that exceeds the person's resources and coping mechanisms (Gilliland and James, 1997)

A conceptual model for understanding tragedy and pain

CHANGE (Tragedy)--------------LOSS-------------PAIN--------------
Stress (perception) (resistance) (anticipation)

Goal of Crisis Intervention

Crisis Counseling differs from other forms of counseling in the following terms:

1. Primary goal to restore the client to equilibrium (may be brief)
2. A second goal of taking action (may be directive and allow temporary client dependency)
3. The counselor takes more active role in giving information and teaching coping strategies

Role of the Crisis Intervener

1. Remove distracters and other stressors
2. Avoid impulsive action
3. Delegate authority
4. Model calmness
5. Be prepared

Crisis Intervention Principles

1. Begin immediately
2. Be concerned and competent
3. Listen to the facts of the situation
4. Reflect the individual's feelings
5. Help the child realize that the crisis event has occurred
6. Do not encourage or support blaming
7. Do not give false reassurance
8. Recognize the primacy of taking action

Crisis Interveners Assessment

Assessing mental statues and functioning
Assessing severity of crisis (cognitive, affective, psychomotor)
Assessing the current emotional status (acute or chronic, person's reservoir of emotional strength)
Assessing alternatives, coping mechanisms, support systems and other resources
Assessing for suicide potential

Crisis Intervener's Action Strategies

Recognize individual differences
Assess your self (values, readiness, physical and emotional limitations)
Show regard for others safety
Provide support
Define the problem clearly
Consider the alternatives
Plan action steps
Use the person's coping strengths
Attend to their immediate needs
Use referral resources
Develop and use networks
Get a commitment

Steps of Crisis Intervention

1. Defining the Problem
2. Ensuring their Safety
3. Providing Support
4. Examine Alternatives
5. Making Plans
6. Obtaining Commitment

Crisis Intervention with the Children

Don'ts and Dos

Do Not

* underestimate children's' ability to feel like adults
* say "everything will be all right. Let's be brave."
*say "stop crying, it can not change things"
*refuse to answer questions
*diverting conversations
*give advice to escape or speed up the processes

DO

* Let the children know they are not alone. I am here for you and with you." to balance the magical and ego-centered thinking and restore some sense of control through outside help

* watch for their physical reactions/symptoms

* communicate creatively (body, tone, eye, touch, play, art, music, etc.)

* understand the children's immature, self centered ways of thinking

* Permit the children to confront (face) losses or other issues

* Explain grief intervention creatively, and translate grief reactions and stages into child-appropriate language. For example:

Denial: I did not want this to happen.
Anger: Why me? It is not fair.
Bargaining: Only if----, may be it would have happened.
Depression: I am not worth living. XXX was such a good person and he died anyway.
Panic: I must do--- in order to survive.
Guilt: I would rather it was me who died.
Worry: I want to do what ever I can to prevent this from happening again.

* help them understand what happened and how they are involved and most importantly, how the are feeling

* understand children react differently in different development stages

More tips for counselors/chaplains/case managers

*Provide honest information and help children master the facts of their existence
*Develop/teach a vocabulary of feelings and thoughts about loss and its resolution
*Parents/teachers should examine their own ideas and unresolved issues related to death and loss
*Provide/discuss adult perspective on the facts of loss
*Help children to anticipate difficult times, holidays like Chinese New Year, birthdays and the anniversary of the tragedy.

Tips for parents

* try all of the above
* Help your child understand what happened
* Talk with the child about the damages, deaths, and traumatic reactions she/her witnessed or sees on TV
* accept and teach the child to express feelings
* listen to the children if he/she shares concerns of her/his peers in the classroom or school.
* keep lines of communication open with the child-even when it is difficult.
* Be involved in the child's school life and understand/request appropriate supports offered by the school and teachers
* work with the child's school to make it more responsive to students in a time of rehabilitation.
* volunteer to work with support groups concerned about the adjustments
* find out what is available in your community for psychological help
* talk with the parents of the child's friends. Discuss how you could form a team to mutually support the children.
* be aware when you need to seek help for your self

Tips for the Children

* work with everyone and make the home a "warm home" to welcome the new children
* listen to them if they share troubling feelings or thoughts. Encourage them to talk to parents and counselors.
* volunteer to be a helper for the new child
* express care, warmth and love for the new children. Be careful about asking too many questions about their sad situations, teasing and intimidating them

Tips for training other personnel

* Provide a written small pamphlet to inform them about the do's and don'ts in responding the children needs
* provide in-service to help them deal with their reactions and coping
* Provide training to better help the children

* For junior high and high school ages, training on watching for early singes of suicide
* establish a referral resources in the immediate community.

Emotional First Aid – Hope for Tomorrow

Emotional First Aid: A set of *life skills,* used by *citizens* and *emergency responders,* to provide the support a person who is *emotionally* shocked, needs *immediately,* following a crisis event.

How to Help the Emotionally Injured After Tragedy Strikes

1. **Reach Out Physically**

    - Position yourself at the victim's side and at his level.
    - Touch - unless the victim pulls away
    - Use a soft voice
    - Use the victim's name

2. **Reach Out Emotionally**

    - Ask the victim how he is feeling
    - Acknowledge the victim's experience
    - Don't minimize the victim's experience (i.e., "You'll be O.K.")

3. **Don't Overlook the Quiet Victims**

    - Many victims after a tragic event are stunned and may appear unaffected. Remember that many people can be affected by a tragic event - witnesses, rescuers, children . . .
    - Don't overlook these "invisible victims"
    - When you suspect someone is affected by a tragic event, reach out with Caring Curiosity — "How are you?"

4. **Protect** the victim from making impulsive decisions. Most major decisions can wait until the victim is thinking clearly.

    - Protect the victims from being victimized by others who may not have the best interest of the victim in mind.
    - Provide for the victim's physical needs - food, medicine, safe place . . .

5. **Reassure:** Many victims have an urgent need for information after a tragic event — "What happened?"; "Why?" Assist the victim in getting the information he needs. The victim may need an Information Advocate.

    - Victims often blame themselves for the crisis event. Help a guilty victim gain perspective by asking him to tell you the "whole story."

    - Try to gently point out to the victim what he did right before, during, or after the tragic event.

6. **Organize:** Victims are often paralyzed after a tragic event and often lose their capacity to deal with all of the new demands created by the tragedy. Assist the victim in developing a simple plan. Suggest — "Let's focus on what needs to be done now."

7. **Reinforce** the actions which the victim is taking or wants to take to emotionally survive the tragic event. The victim will struggle to find something or someone to hold onto in the first few hours. You may need to "clear the way" so that what the victim wants to do he is able to do.

8. **Summary:** In the first few hours after a tragic event, the victim is often surrounded by people who have "a job to do" or who have opinions about what the victim should or shouldn't do. The primary goal of the person providing Emotional First Aid is to enable the victim to act according to his wishes, values, and beliefs and not according to what others think should be done.

    - Do not "overcare" or do too much for the victim. Remember that the primary psychological challenge for the victim is to regain a sense of control. Therefore, the victim should be encouraged to make decisions and take action in his own behalf.

    - Finally, a broken heart cannot "be fixed." Don't try! A caring presence is what you can offer to someone who is emotionally devastated. Just being there is very powerful and will be experienced by the victim as very helpful.

What To Say

- "What happened?"
- "I'm so sorry"

What Not To Say

- "I know how you feel"
- "Calm down"
- "Don't cry"

- “This must be very difficult for you”
- “It’s O.K. to feel . . . “
- “I don’t know what to say”
- “It could be worse”
- “God has his reasons”

Crisis Response Services

CRISIS CAN HAPPEN AT

ANYTIME

David J Fair, D. Min. Executive Director

Everyone needs to call for backup every now and then!

Providing Psychological Services, Professional Debriefing, Consultation, and Pastoral Care for all Public Safety Personnel and their Families.

Officers, EMT's, Doctors, Nurses, Firefighters, Chaplains any Responder

We also provide fee-based training in a variety of areas such as stress management, anger management, mental health intervention, mental status evaluations, suicidal assessment, chaplaincy program development and other topics upon request.

http://www.crisis-chaplain.org/index.html

DEPLOYMENT HISTORY OF SOME OF OUR STAFF

Luby's Massacre at Killeen, Texas Oklahoma City Bombing* Ground Zero - 911 Branch Dividian, Waco* East Texas Columbia Shuttle Disaster * Debriefed Debriefers * CISM/CISD

Green Cross Assistance

Sri Lanka, Tsunami Deployment

Dave Fair's Experience
As Deputy Incident Commander

Overview

The Tsunami that struck Southeast Asia in December '04 was devastating to a number of third world countries, already dealing with shaky economies and political woes.

There was an explosion of groups rushing to aid, quickly running advertisements to urge people to give. Some of these organizations self deployed, never a "best practice".

Green Cross Assistance was invited to respond to Sri Lanka via Sri Lanka Cricket.

It became very obvious, that one must only respond by invitation. Green Cross has always done this.

In 1991 in Killeen, Texas following the Luby's Massacre several groups self deployed and it created problems for all groups as well as those officers and civilians being assisted.

The same has been true with Oklahoma City, Columbine, Wedgwood, and 911.

It is clear that Green Cross adheres to the standard of responding by request only.

We developed three teams, but only two were deployed.

Above: Dave Fair, at Green Cross Deputy Incident Command in Texas

Kathy Figley was serving as Incident Commander and when she deployed to Sri Lanka. Sam and I served as Deputy Incident Commanders.

Challenges

It must be noted this was Green Cross's first international deployment. Regardless of a few bumps in the road, it is clear, based on both after action reports and correspondence from the Sri Lankan's, the project was a tremendous success.

Lessons Learned

- Don’t try to use Pay Pal oversees.
- Money is also hard to wire
- Insist on members completing pre deployment questionnaire
- Appoint a mediator
- Establish a petty cash fund for team leaders
- They don’t get our jokes
- Be keenly aware of cultural diversity
- Oil and water don’t mix, neither do some personalities

Conclusion

Most if not all of my comments relate to the operations end of the process. I am sure those on the ground will have good input on suggestions from their vantage point. I am so pleased Kathy was able to deploy and get a first hand look at the on the ground operation. That proved invaluable to us.

This was a tremendous learning experience for me personally and I appreciate the opportunity to serve. My thanks to Charles, Kathy, Karen, Sam, Marie, and anyone else I may have forgotten on the I/C team. Special thanks to the team leaders and members.

Deployment Protocol and Gate Keeper Criteria for Brownwood Crisis Trauma Team

1.1 HISTORY AND RATIONAILE

It is evident from previous disasters both natural and man made that there needs to be some management of the persons who respond to offer spiritual and psychological support.

While most people are well meaning, without proper training and experience they can re traumatize the very people they wish to help.

As a secondary issue, there have been instances where reporters, lawyers, and souvenir seekers posed as members of the clergy to obtain access to the scene.

Lastly even if persons are qualified, the number of people having access to victims and family members must be limited as victims and families can easily be over whelmed.

Therefore it is imperative that immediately after the incident and for the first 72 hours, there be a screening and credentialing procedure to manage individuals or groups wanting to offer spiritual or other support.
This protocol is written with this in mind.

1.2 AUTHORITY:

The authority to set up a deployment protocol, procedures for quality control of spiritual and psycho local services, and credential gate keeping is granted to the Brownwood Police Chaplain Division, which is the sponsoring organization for the Brownwood Crisis Trauma Team (CISD/CISM), and the SMART Team. Authority is granted by the City Of Brownwood, Emergency Operations Division.

There shall be four components of the overall management of these services:

1. **Agency Chaplains-** those providing services to their agencies and the public at large.

2. **SMART Team**- Providing Spiritual and Psychological Services through trained Certified Crisis Clergy and trained Certified Crisis Mental Health Professionals

3. **Brownwood Crisis Trauma Team-** Providing CISM services.

4. **Pre approved Providers**

MHMR
Red Cross
Baptist Men
Salvation Army
Green Cross

1.3 TRAINING REQUIRMENTS

1. **Agency Chaplains-** Basic ICISF, Pastoral Crisis Intervention- Certified Crisis Clergy- Hold at least a Senior Chaplain Certification from the ICPC.

2. **SMART Team-**

Clergy: a minimum of Certified Crisis Clergy, Ecclesiastical endorsement or equal from religious organization

Mental Health Professional: A Texas State License in counseling, marriage and family therapy, social work, or chemical dependency, plus Certified Crisis Mental Health Professional

3. ***Brownwood Crisis Trauma Team-*** Minimum of ICISF Basic CISM and one additional ICISF level

4. ***Pre*** approved Providers- Minimum training required by their organization for disaster work

5. Outside Assistance-

For intervention services only: Outside assistance will be accepted only from bona fide CISD/CISM teams, who are either part of The Texas Dept. Of Health CISM Network, the Texas DPS Peer Support Team, or on the ICISF International Registry.

For Mental Health Services: Outside assistance will only be accepted from MHMR Crisis Teams, NOVA Teams, or other bona fide groups that can provide a letter from their city, county or other creditable source attesting to their competency in disaster work.

Notice: No individual self dispatched clergy or mental health workers will be credentialed.

1.4 **CREDENTIALING:**

All persons who are part of the disaster response who are approved for service will be issued a City of Brownwood Incident Identification. This must be worn at all times on site, at triage areas, and family centers.

> In addition to the Brownwood I.D., each person will be issued a Daily Site ID. This ID will change color each day, and must be worn with the Brownwood I.D.
>
> Persons not wearing the Brownwood I.D. and/or the appropriate color of the day ID will be removed from service

1.5 REPORTING FOR DUTY

Activation for local teams will be made through the normal activation process. There will be assignments made primarily to Brownwood Regional Medical Center waiting rooms, on site patient triage areas, temporary morgues, and family assistance centers.

Activation of out of area services will be made by contacting the Texas Department of Health, DPS CIRT Austin, ICISC, NOVA, or other similar groups.

Resources, will be explained to these groups, and they will be asked to report back within the hour, as to what is available.

Red Cross, Salvation Army, and MHMR will be notified and placed on stand by. In addition Red Cross will mobilize a single SRV to provide initial nourishment at the demobilization area.

Incident Command:

The Director of Chaplain Services /CISM Coordinator or his designee will report to the Incident Command Center. The IC structure will be utilized for each event.

All persons who have been assigned duties and/or shifts will report to the staging area 15 minutes before start of shift for a briefing.

All persons, whose shift is ending, must go through the demobilization before leaving for the day.

At the end of each person's tour of duty they must go through an exit debriefing.

Crisis Response Chaplain Services
104 East Industrial Drive
Early, Texas 76802

The Crisis Response Chaplain Services office is located in the Early (Texas) Chamber of Commerce and Early Small Business Incubator Building. The above photo is an outside view of the building where our office is located.

www.crisis-chaplain.org

Chaplain Dave Fair, along with Chaplain Leatha Warden, LPC provide services through Crisis Response Chaplain Services, and Fair, Warden and Associates.
The Chaplaincy responds to responder crisis, while the pair also operates a separate counseling, and consulting service for the public.

Police Chaplain Letter to the Editor - Police Memorial Week

May 9th through the 15th is National Law Enforcement Week, with May 15th as Police Memorial Day, honoring officers who have been killed in the line of duty.

Locally the Brownwood City Council and the Brown County Commissioners Court have passed resolutions recognizing that week, and paying tribute to all our local police officers.

Brownwood and Brown County are fortunate to have dedicated officers who place their life on the line every day to protect and to serve us.

Officers are officers 24/7. Even if they are out with their family at a restaurant, attending a movie, or in their personal car, they are still officers. There is no extra pay for this, just extra danger. I have seen officers get out of their own car and send their families down the road so they could intervene.

Officers miss birthday parties, little league games, and Christmas dinner, because their departments are manned 24/7. I have seen officers wade through the mud in freezing temperatures or direct traffic when its 108 degrees.

One of the sad things about our officers is they usually have to work lots of overtime or a second job to make ends meet. Traditionally departments tend to be understaffed and under paid.

Our local officers are out standing men and women. Please take time to thank them for what they do for us. Thank the civilian employees too. The communication operators, jailers, secretarial staff. All of them make a great contribution to the cause.

I am proud to have the honor of working with these truly outstanding individuals.

Chaplain Dave Fair, Brownwood Police Dept.

You Made a Difference

As I look back over my life there are people who made a real difference.

Eugene Ingram

Although dying of cancer, Gene showed me courage, and how to love people, how to give to others. There was nothing this man wouldn't do for you. And then quietly, in his own way he would give credit to God for anything good he did. I first saw Jesus in him.

Jane Huff

My 6th grade school teacher at Southwest Elementary School in Brownwood, Texas. She gave good advice, taught me to help others, and to tend to my own knitting.

Mary Michaels

My 8th grade teacher at Brownwood Jr. High. Got me interested in radio broadcasting at 13. My career spanned 30 years and I became President of Texas Associated Broadcasters Association.

Ted Kell

Minister, Austin Avenue Church of Christ, Brownwood, Texas. A true Chaplain's Chaplain. One of the best men I ever knew.

Captain/Inspector Ron Snow

Captain, Texas Department of Public Safety. Encouraged me to join the Texas DPS Chaplain Program. Taught me in the law enforcement academy, when I decided to attend, at 48, with guys twice my size and half my age. A man true to his word. He taught us integrity.

And there are others, Dr. Dan, Chaplain Leatha, My Mom and Dad. My daughters, my granddaughters. My brother Ed.

WE OFFER A SAFE PLACE IN THE "EYE OF THE STORM"

For Public Safety Professionals and Their Families

CRITICAL INCIDENT STRESS DEBRIEFING

Critical Incident Stress Debriefing (CISD) is a group technique used after a critical incident. It is designed to minimize the impact of that event and to aid the recovery of people who have been exposed to disturbing events. Critical Incident Stress Debriefings were designed by Dr. Jeffrey T. Mitchell, of the University of Maryland, to prevent post-traumatic stress among high-risk occupational groups. Initially developed for firefighters, paramedics and police officers, use of the Mitchell Model has been modified and expanded for use in natural disasters, school-based incidents, and a variety of other settings.

Stress Management

Police officers and rescue workers in general, share personality traits that can feed into the stress of a critical incident. Personality factors of Law Enforcement Personnel include:

* A need to be in control
* Obsessive/ perfectionist tendencies
* Compulsive/traditional values -- wanting things to remain unchanged
* High levels of internal motivation
* Action-oriented
* High need for stimulation and excitement (easily bored)
* High need for immediate gratification
* Tendency to take risks

* Highly dedicated
* Invested in the job due to months of training and preparation , view job as life long career
* Identify strongly with their role as a police officer
* High need to be needed

Post-Shooting Trauma Intervention

For many years health professionals have recognized the emotional and psychological impact that can result in the aftermath of life threatening catastrophic events. Over the last several decades, however, this phenomenon has been brought to wider public attention in large measure by the significant number of Vietnam veterans who have suffered adverse and sometimes severe emotional reactions to their wartime experiences - in many cases, years after they had returned from combat.

These and other factors have increased our understanding and appreciation of the psychological and emotional effects on survivors of traumatic violence and death in a variety of contexts. The psychological effects sometimes suffered by victims of kidnap, rape, or assault, as well as victims of airline hijackings and crashes, for example, are generally referred to as critical incident trauma or post traumatic stress disorders (PTSD).

In spite of the fact that police officers are trained to recognize and deal with a variety of violent and traumatic circumstances, they also often fall victim to such stress disorders.

The context for most of these disorders revolves around shooting incidents wherein an officer shoots someone and/or is shot, or witnesses the shooting or killing of another officer or individual. Post-shooting trauma incorporates a range of stress-induced reactions which have been broadly defined and examined for a number of years. It should be recognized that police-involved shootings are not the only situation which can be defined as critical incidents.

CISM Services for all public safety agencies are offered. This process is designed to return personnel to their pre-crisis level of functioning and to normalize the incident. Stress Management training specifically designed for police, fire and EMS is offered for academies, in service schools, individual agencies and departments.

Assistance is available for officers involved in shooting incidents. The PSTT (Post Shooting Trauma Team) is available to respond to support officers and their families

CRISIS CAN HAPPEN AT ANYTIME!

Officers, EMT's, Doctors, Nurses, Firefighters,
Any Responder

CALL FOR PRAYER 24 / 7 - 325-647-7171

Nothing in these pages is to be substituted for the consultation and care of a doctor. Always contact your doctor with any questions. Chest Pain can signal a critical illness. **Call 911**.

Grief by Any Other Name is Still Grief

Elizabeth Kubler- Ross: The Stages of Death and Dying

(1) Denial and Isolation

(2) Anger

(3) Bargaining

(4) Depression

(5) Acceptance

Granger Westburg from Good Grief

(1) Shock

(2) Express Emotion

(3) Depressed and Lonely

(4) Panicky

(5) Since of Guilt

(6) Anger and Resentment

(7) Resist returning

(8) Gradually Hope Abides

(9) Struggle to Affirm Reality

June Cerza Kolf: When Will I Stop Hurting

(1) Shock

(2) Sighing

(3) Crying

(4) Anger

(5) Depression

(6) Final Stage

A. Growth
B. Return
C. Reaching Out To Others

Dave Fair: On Traumatic Death

(1) Stunned, Shock

(2) Strong Emotions

(3) Questions / Guilt (The If Onlys)

(4) Confusion

(5) Obsession / Compulsion

(6) Emotional Shut Down (Just prior to funeral)

(7) Fear, Anxiety and Loneliness (when people leave)

(8) Anger and Depression

(9) Searching / Reaching Out

(10) A New Normal

"My peace I leave with you"

I could see the lights flashing on the patrol cars from blocks away as I sped to the old north side water tower. Must be 150 feet in the air. Parking just outside the police yellow barrier tape, a young police officer met me. "He had a fight with his girl friend. They broke up", he shouted over the noise, pointing upward to the small figure of a teenager on the rail of the old water tower.

Working my way to the fence surrounding the tower, it was locked. "Get a fire unit here, "I shouted to the officer, "We need them to cut the lock. Got to get under the tower if I'm going to talk to him ", I added.

I wondered what God had in mind to reach the distressed young man, what ever it was I prayed it would work.

The officer called dispatch and then introduced a fail man in his 60's identified as the boy's father. "He is 16. Told me they had a fight", the father said. "Told me he was gonna kill himself" he tearfully concluded.

The fire-rescue truck arrived and the Captain made quick work of getting me inside the gate. Climbing up the latter a few feet, "Can you hear me "I screamed up to the boy. He moved around the railing, although I couldn't make out his face he about half waved a hand.

"We need to get you down from there so we can talk. Will you come down"? I asked. The youth replied no. "If anyone tried to get me I'll jump," adding he wanted to die and life was not worth living if he couldn't be with his girl friend. "Would you come down if the three of us could sit and talk about this", I yelled back.

The frightened boy told me he might come down if she would talk to him when he did.

I asked the father if he had the girls name and number. He did. Calling the girl on the cell phone, she had no idea what had been going on. I told her not to come at this point. "Can't run the risk of you exciting him and then him jumping. " I told her. "Stay home. When I get him down I'll call you to meet us".

After some 15 minutes of negotiating the boy agreed to climb down. Carefully I watched along with others as he started down one step at a time. He fell into my arms sobbing. "The worst is over son", I told him, putting my arm around him. His Dad embraced both of us.

"Let's go get a cup of coffee ", I said, adding, "God is not through with you yet".

The boy was pleased his girl friend would talk to him and I hit redial on the cell phone handing it to him.

"Hi", he told her. "I'm ok. This guy got me down. Yeah it's gonna be ok." he concluded.

Voicing a silent prayer of thanksgiving we headed for the coffee shop. God had again spares a life.

Photo by Hal Stoelzle - Rocky Mountain News

Musings

It strains your soul....

To enter this black hole, this awesome empty moment in time where there is no life, no apparent hope, no clear meaning and seeks to encounter those whose world just know shatters into endless splintered slivers of disconnected

We seek to be there and the scene when it is ugliest not later when the dirty work is done.

Wounds, tears, and shreds folk's souls

A task despicable but must be done with love. Make no mistake about it such work wounds the soul.

Don't just do something stand there.

Death is so very quiet

Grieve, hurt, process, remember

Ministry of listening, presents, and availability

Our own private "once upon a time" moments of sadness and sorrow.

These too deserve care
Mental survival

Carry on where others must leave to return to duty

Individual disasters almost daily
For most it's once in a lifetime and one time too much

Unknown

Only God Knows

I wonder how many dead babies I have seen.

How many broken bodies.

Broken minds.

Broken hearts.

I wonder how many tears I have seen shed.

How many I have shed.

How many AIDS patients I have known.

Blood.

Pain.

Death.

Hurt.

Will it ever stop?

When is enough, enough?

You can't swim in the sewer without getting some on you.

So easy to become cynical.

God cries too

Joel Stein

Maintaining Religious Neutrality in Crisis With Out Compromising Your Own Beliefs

For The Victim

- **Victims are already in a spiritual crisis**
- **God talk can re-traumatize victims**

For The Therapist

- **Therapists must be comfortable with the victim's secular or religious outlook**
- **Therapists must be able to "read" the lay of the spiritual land**
- **Thou shall not be shocked. There are dozens of "religions".**
- **Therapists must be stable in their own religious views**
- **Therapists must seek what ever they need to feed their spirit when on deployment**

For The Compassion Fatigue Specialist

- **Must be sensitive to the therapists religious bent**
- **Must be familiar with general religious buzz words and trappings**
- **Must be able to mirror back to therapist encouragement and comfort using similar verbiage**
- **Thou shall not be shocked. There are dozens of "religions".**

For the Incident Commander

- **Must be in tune with I/C staff to pick up on "spiritual trauma"**
- **Must be able to refer I/C member as necessary to approprate CFS for support**

For Application in Sri Lanka Deployment

For The Victims

- **Existing problems with groups attempting to "convert" population**
- **Local mainline ministers trying to maintain a fine line of balance**
- **At least one group going to a camp with "religious intent" stoned by some camp dwellers**

For Deployed GSP Members

- **What can and can't be said of a religious nature to victims**
- **How to refuel their own spirituality while deployed**
- **Rituals theirs and ours**

COPS and COLLARS, MENTAL HEALTH CRISIS TEAM

JOINS WITH POLICE CHAPLAINS FOR NEW PROGRAM

It's 3:30 AM, and I fumble for the phone. The police dispatcher tells me there is a woman at a local restaurant talking to herself and tearing up napkins.

I'm on call. I slip on my clothes already laid out, jump in my car and call dispatch on the radio that I'm on my way.

I arrive, park out of the way next to a police unit already there. Slipping into the restaurant, I spot an older women sitting in a back booth. Two coffee cups are on the table, and she is shredding napkins into little pieces all the while talking to someone that is not there.

As a law enforcement Chaplain over 15 years, I have seen humanity at its worst and it's best. I've been no stranger to death and destruction, to mayhem and tragedy.

Having made hundreds of death notifications, comforted grieving widows, and calmed crying children; most mental health issues are relatively new to me.

Mental Health Chaplaincy has been around a long time. The very first Clinical Pastoral Education (CPE) was started by a minister in a psychiatric hospital setting, who himself was a patient suffering from mental illness. Wayne E. Oates, and after his death his institute carried the concept forward and today is still a driving force.

While mental health Chaplaincy is strong today, it is found mostly in institutions. Interestingly enough while the separation of church and state battle goes on, in Texas, there are full time paid Chaplains in all state hospitals, paid with tax dollars.

What is new to mental health Chaplaincy is the Chaplain responding to crisis's in the field. In Brownwood, Texas, a unique alliance has been formed between Central Texas MHMR and the Chaplain Services Unit of the Brownwood Police Department.

While the Brownwood protocol for the last 15 years calls for a Chaplain to be dispatched on attempted suicides, the model has been expanded.

During the last Texas legislative session, law makers adopted a major over haul of the states mental health system, the resulting funding cuts, have caused services to be scaled back. This is where the alliance of mental health professionals and Chaplains came together.

Locally MHMR maintained a 24-hour crisis line, and a crisis team responds to appropriate crisis situations. Additionally the Crisis Team responds to calls on mental health emergencies from police and EMS, and lastly serves the county jail on suicide watch and the hospital ER for a host of issues.

After hours, on weekends and holidays, MHMR has only one crisis worker for 7 counties. So Ghasem Navapour, MHMR Executive Director and Dave Fair, Director of Chaplain Services for the Brownwood Police Dept., developed a protocol, training schedule and implementation for the Police Chaplains. With the blessings of Police Chief Virgil Cowin, the program was implemented January 1, 2004.

Brownwood Police Chaplains now serve as "first responders" for the MHMR Crisis Team during the hours and day's only one crisis worker is on call. If a law enforcement officer calls for the Crisis Team, or if someone calls the 24 hours crisis line, and are in crisis the Chaplain is dispatched.

The final training before the program kicked off was with Kerrville State Hospital. There were matters of procedure and law needing to be covered.

The Chaplains also are taking the Mental Health Peace Officer certification course from the state. Although all are not commissioned officers the training is invaluable.

To date the Chaplains have responded to over 150 mental health emergencies for MHMR. Of that number some are resolved in the field as a result of crisis intervention. 50 of the persons were admitted to psychiatric hospitals, mostly state facilities. The balance were admitted to local hospitals, the MHMR Respite, or sent home with family members.

Many of the cases involve suicide ideology; others are dual diagnosis, where alcohol or drugs are involved. The Chaplains feel fortunate. Through training and intervention no patients have been lost in the first six months of the program.

The Chaplains and MHMR crisis workers mesh well. Better than most thought. The key was both groups have been working the streets, seeing the same people, and sometimes collaborating.

How are the patients and their families reacting to Chaplains? Excellent. For one thing the Chaplains dress down. No police uniform, no shinny badges. The Chaplain could easily be someone's dad or mom.

In addition to subtle dress, most patients have a since that a clergyman can help even if they don't know how. There is a calming presents that the Chaplain brings.

There are times the Chaplain becomes unpopular. On a recent case involving a schizophrenic, the woman became angry with the Chaplain when she was told a trip to the local hospital was necessary. In Texas Emergency Detention Orders signed by a judge work just like a warrant. It is explained to patients in most cases they can go voluntarily ridding with the Chaplain. But if they refuse an ED is obtained and an officer transports them to the ER.

The public seems happy with the crisis worker Chaplain marriage. The Chaplains fill the void left by funding cuts, and are on duty anyway. It then becomes a short hop from there to a mental health emergency.

There have been cases where two patients were presenting at different locations. So a second Chaplain is sometimes called out, when the calls are backing up.

One of the things that prepared the Chaplains for mental health work involved FBI hostage negotiation training they received. All the

Brownwood Chaplains are FBI trained, and that training is helpful in suicide intervention.

One of the Chaplains, also a deputy sheriff, and another Chaplain a Licensed Professional Counselor, serve as negotiators for the Sheriff's Office SWAT Team. Learning how to make a "hip pocket" diagnosis so you know how to interact with the subject is great groundwork for other mental health emergencies.

Based on the protocol Chaplains contact the person in crisis, face to face. If the Chaplain can defuse the crisis in the field using crisis intervention techniques, there is no need for further action at that time. The Chaplains FAX paper work to MHMR and a follow up is done.

If the crisis is such that it is likely a commitment to a psychiatric hospital will be needed, the Chaplain attempts to get the person to voluntarily go with them to the local hospital emergency room for medical clearance.

In the meantime the Chaplain briefs the on call crisis worker. If it's decided that an emergency detention is needed to send the person to a psychiatric hospital, the Chaplain begins the paper work and the MHMR worker comes to the hospital to finish it up from the clinician side.

A magistrate is called to sign the order and the Chaplain notifies the Brown County Sheriff's Department that a transport deputy will be needed. In Texas the sheriff has the responsibility to transport patients to state hospitals if a court order has been issued.

Occasionally a person in crisis doesn't fit the standard mold. Staying at home may be out of the question, but the criteria for a state hospital stay are not met. In those cases the Chaplain, with the consent of the crisis worker, can take the person to the MHMR Respite Center. There the patient can be watched and helped by trained staff.

Ready to kick off the final six months of the year the Chaplains continue to train and to interact with the Crisis Workers. A monthly meeting at MHMR between caseworkers, police officers, deputies and Chaplains is a great forum for reviewing cases and new ideas.

All in all the Chaplains and MHMR are given high marks for the new and innovative program.

When Our Helping Turns To Hurting-
Keeping Ourselves and Those We Help On Track

When an officer has been around a shooting or similar critical incident, he or she wants to talk about the event in terms other officers can relate to. Even lesser traumatic events become war stories.

However if the officer was personally impacted by the event, most choose to sidestep discussions about that part of the incident. Most anyone who has been traumatized tends to stay away from the worst part of the incident. It is very uncomfortable often filled *with sheer terror. When we veer away, it is called, "stuffing down", or suppressing.*

Yet at the appropràte time the officer needs to recall those thoughts, feelings and emotions as part of the emotional healing process.

But what if the Chaplain ***unknowingly steers the officer away*** from what is helpful? From what needs to be talked about, vented? How could that happen?

We must remember as Chaplain's we have seen and heard heavy doses of grief, tragedy, and trauma in our job. In addition for those Chaplains who pastor they have the added weight of the church to deal with. That's a pretty heavy load. To top it all off, we have likely been involved ourselves in critical incidents. So we know first hand what it is like to shy away from thinking about or talking about curtain events or issues.

When you couple the stress on an officer with trauma the Chaplain may be harboring it can be a recipe for disaster.

Because everyone may be "on their last nerve", including the Chaplain, sometime we tend to guide the officer away from the subject at hand that needs to be talking about, explored.

If the Chaplain's "gunny sack" is full and we feel we just can't take any more, subconsciously we may be veering the officer we are trying to help away from his trauma.

Chaplains, because of our own unresolved trauma may be so uncomfortable with the way conversation is going, that we change the direction of the discussion sometimes without realizing it.

If Chaplains are not aware of this point it can cause them to do more harm than good while trying to help officers and victims,

Here is a checklist to use to find out if you should back out. The list can help determine if you are negatively reacting to a conversation. It is a red flag that can alert you prior to veering off path, taking the officer with you.

(1) Are you becoming more uncomfortable with the conversation the closer it comes to the worst part of the trauma?

(2) If you are meeting with the officer several times, do you find yourself dreading the next meeting?

(3) During discussion of the trauma do you find yourself either becoming angry or blaming the officer's actions for the bad part that happened?

(4) During the conversation are physical symptoms, you don't normally notice manifesting themselves?

(5) Are "issues" arising during the conversation you aren't usually concerned with?

(6) Did you have a flash back, or a "rerun" of some past event in your life?

(7) Are you experiencing a "free floating anxiety", you can't tie to something specific in your current life. ?

If any of these things red flag, you should immediately take a break to collect your thoughts. There is an important choice to make at this time.

Are you able to recognize what is happing to you? If so are you ok with forging ahead being careful not to let the conversation veer off track? Are you able to return to the discussion?

If in fact the discussion has triggered something in you, it may be advisable for you not to continue. The first law of being a Chaplain has to do with your own safety physically and psychologically. You must take care of yourself. Even if you are aware of what is happening, but you feel an accelerated amount of stress, you are wise to back out. There is no sin in letting someone else work with this officer or victim.

How does a Chaplain keep this "veering into the bar ditch" from developing? The first thing we must do is deal with our own trauma. There are likely chronic issues from the past, these may take longer to address in a healthy manner, but new critical incidents as we experience them should be dealt with right away.

I wrote an article several years ago called Chaplain Cumulative Stress Syndrome.(ICPC Newsletter) I pointed out Chaplains not only experience trauma just as officers do, they also hear a lot of second hand trauma. Add that to normal situations you deal with in public ministry and you have a heavy load to bear.

It is important to understand, chaplains act as shock absorbers. Tending to absorb all of the impacts of everyone else's trauma, yet you can't pass it on.

As a result, if Chaplains don't empty their "gunny sacks" on a regular basis they are heading for an emotional meltdown.

Chaplains who are directly involved in an incident must not participate as a debriefer or peer in debriefings, defusing, or similar interventions conducted as a result of the incident. This is a major mistake that is made. It re-traumatizes the Chaplain.

At Ground Zero after 911, Chaplains were not allowed on the pile for any reason other than to pray for remains. We were not to become part of the search or recovery operation.

It is important for everyone's mental and spiritual health to deal with our traumas.

Chaplains need a Chaplain and should know when to refer ourselves to another Chaplain, or mental health professional. When we continue to experience reactions even after we have self terminated working with the officer, then something else may be going on.

We all need to keep the "well water" clean. Running water tends to stay much cleaner. So if we are venting and moving forward ourselves, that's great. But if we get stagnant and dam up the flow, we have poisoned our own well water, and anyone drinking from it becomes "infected" from our own trauma. We contaminate anyone we try to help.

In Texas those of us who are Chaplains for the Texas Department of Public Safety, Critical Incident Team, are able to seek out the department's staff psychologist Dr. Frances Douglas. She has been a great help to those of us needing to empty our "gunny sack"

Don't complicate someone else's trauma. Don't make yours worse. Seek out a competent professional for yourself when needed.

Sobriety and Recovery- It's Rarely Back and White
Is the Church Failing It's Members?

The meeting attendee was on a roll, "Bill needs to know it is a sin to drink, God forgives but it's still a sin". I glanced at another man in the group, a recovering alcoholic and drug addict. He was sadly shaking his head. We had talked many times before. I knew what he was thinking, "great hit them in the head with a 40 pound King James Bible that ought to fix everything." I knew in his recovery he had been hurt deeply by the pastor of his church.

Fact is the Bible talks about sin and drinking but not in the same verse. Actually the text reads that drunkenness is sin.

The Apostle Paul talked about the war between our members. In other words our battle within. A battle that rages every bit as hard as the battle between, clergy and clinicians.
Addiction. Is it sin? Is it disease?
Or is it neither or maybe both.

Those quick to call any addiction sin point to the disease concept as an excuse, some way to justify what a person is doing. I heard a minister once say, "If you let them call it a disease, it's just a license to sin". My response was, "they don't need a license, they are going to drink anyway."

In his recent book, Eddie Russell, fmi, writes, Sickness and disease came through sin in the first place. *(Catechism of the Catholic Church. 1505/440).* Sin came into the world in the beginning through Adam after he believed Satan's lies. With that lie came sin and every degree of filth, fear and death. Every sickness and disease is a degree of death because it robs us of life and, if we get sick enough, we die. From the very beginning Satan was on the scene to lie, to kill and to steal God's gifts from man. No sooner than God had spoken the Word, Satan was ready to rob Adam and Eve of God's abundance and purpose for their lives.

I used to smile at the softball fields on balmy Texas summer evenings. It was church league season. You could usually tell the denomination by what was in the back of the pick-up trucks. The Methodists and Catholics were likely to have a beer cooler.

Well then, if drinking is a sin, then are those two denominations sinners? But let's see. If one of them offered a beer to an Assembly of God church member, is that a sin? The Bible says, "To cause a brother to stumble" is sin. So let's see now. The Methodist may not be sinning by drinking, if he doesn't get drunk. But if he gets drunk, maybe he sinned. But if he was Catholic maybe it wouldn't be a venereal sin. So if he isn't sinning that's good, and if the Assembly of God member refuses the beer then the Methodist still didn't sin. Yet, it the Assembly of God person drinks the beer then does that make the Methodist a sinner?

Sounds absurd? Yep! It makes as much sense as the debate between sin or disease. The only thing worst is, trying to understand it with a bad hangover as your pastor and therapist duke it out. My point is, things are rarely black and white. Even in the church world.

Why do some religious leaders claim alcoholism is a sin? The Bible does not talk about alcoholism? It does condemn drunkenness yet the closest thing to alcoholism is when the qualifications for elders and overseers are stated in 1 Timothy and Titus "not given too much drink" or "not a lover of strong drink". Actually the Scripture is lacking when it comes to the subject of alcohol. The Bible says that drunkenness is a sin; it should not be automatically assumed that alcoholism is a sin.

There is an overwhelming amount of medical evidence that indicates it is a disease with both physical and mental characteristics. If alcoholism is a sin and a disease how can one repent of a disease? I can see how one can repent of drunkenness, but not a disease. Especially a disease that shows evidence that it is hereditary. Maybe it would be best to treat the disease as a disease and the sin (drunkenness) as a sin.

One has to be very careful about calling alcoholism a sin. We don't want to lump all alcoholics under the umbrella of unrepentant sinners. There are believing Christians who are repentant for their abuse of alcohol. They are alcoholics--addicted to alcohol. They suffer from the abuse of alcohol. That's how they got to be alcoholics. God has forgiven them, and with God's help they have overcome the active practicing of their addiction to alcohol.

Truth be known there is a blending of the sin vs. disease concepts that has resulted in by far the best recovery program known to man. And it's not run by theologians or doctors.

It's run by those who have a vested interest in recovery. It's the AA 12 Step Program. Yes it speaks of addiction as disease. But it also involves the belief and faith in a Higher Power. It is a very Spiritual program, but not a religious one.

With the Bible lacking more specifics, and with alcoholism on the rise among the clergy, many ministers are beginning to earnestly seek answers. Troubled by their dilemma clergy members are seeking answers from the addiction treatment community. In some cases ministers are going through counselor training, while others are in fact attending 12 step meetings. They are learning there is no doubt remission is spiritually oriented.

One cleric states, “I always though those in AA might pray to a “doorknob” as their Higher Power. I was surprised to find many AA members either have or they are seeking a relationship with God

“Literature supports the notion that clinical experience which encourages patients to surrender control to a power outside themselves (AA’s first three steps) is beneficial.

Twelve Step programs have gotten a bad rap from those who have never attended meetings or know the story of the 12 step program roots. Preachers are often shocked to find the genesis of AA had deep spiritual roots. So deep in fact the founders had to lighten up a bit in their selling of the concept to addicts to get them to even listen.

Rather than beat the drunk over the head with the Bible, AA members share their experience, strength and hope with fervor much like an evangelist. They tout AA attendance is linked to better prognosis when treating addiction.

One of the hardest nuts to crack are the old mainline denominationalist who pastor stoic churches and are dogmatic about their belief system. However the proof is in the pudding.

All it requires is one or two addicts who are in recovery, clean and sober, sitting on the front pew Sunday morning. It is those people who are living out their experience, strength, and hope the tenets of AA.

So let the battle rage between the two camps. Perhaps some of us have our "halo" on a bit too tight. Maybe we should ask those in recovery what works and what doesn't.

Even The American Psychological Association, once wary of anything even vaguely religious, has now published a series of scholarly and clinical volumes on the interface of psychology with spirituality and religion. Even in religious circles the pervasiveness of an act that becomes deeply rooted is akin to the disease concept. 3

Lest we never forget the words of the Lord. As children we memorized John 3:16, the salvation verse. But few of us ever read much less committed to memory John 3:17. For God did not send His son into the world to condemn the world, but that it should be saved through him.

If Jesus didn't come into the world to condemn the world, then who am I (therapist, minister, Chaplain, doctor) to condemn it. (Them)

References:

1 (From 12 Steps to Divine Healing by Eddie Russell, fmi)

2 Dr. Darvin Smith, lecture notes and handouts

3 From the Clergy Faces the Addiction Question - Fair

Is It Sin or Disease-

Clergy Faces the Addiction Dilemma

For years the battle over the disease concept has plagued fundamentalist ministers as they struggle with addiction issues in their congregations.

Many clergy have been taught addictions are sins, moral weaknesses. In addition they have been critical of the "higher power" concept in 12 step programs. For seventy years spirituality has been at the heart of the 12-Step program of recovery.

Depending on ministry training and the denominational background of ministers, many have been taught curtain scriptures[4] (Ephesians 5:18 do not get drunk on wine, which leads to debauchery. Instead, be filled with the Spirit.) , point to alcohol consumption as sinful. When faced with parishioners seeking help from them or going into treatment, clergy often find themselves at odds with what is best for the person vs. their own theology.

Alcoholics worry too, as they often report they have suffered some sort of negative experience with religion and many have an image of God as punitive.[1]

For the alcoholic or addict who is in a congregational setting he usually does not want his minister to know of his problem. In the same breath he is cognoscente of the need for some spiritual support.[6] Enter the clergyman knowledgeable about the recovery process. Yet despite increases in educational efforts this type of minister is few and far between.

Clergy who do embrace the recovery community are learning to widen their definition of spirituality. Indeed, a life- enhancing spirituality is a deeply personal dynamic that provides meaning and purpose in life, leads to self-transcendence, and promotes interpersonal connection. Spirituality, for most people, flows from and gives expression to their religious convictions. For others spirituality is not grounded in traditional religious beliefs but is, nonetheless, the expression of their core values and approach to life.[1]

AA‘s approach to spirituality is more a reflection of the broader definition rather than that of religion. However many of their members use their religion to bolster there spiritual experience.

It has been found ministers directly involved in the recovery process as support persons mimic the clinical pastoral counselor’s role in the health care community. Their notion is embrace people of any faith or of no faith.

Troubled by their dilemma clergy members are seeking answers from the addiction treatment community. In some cases ministers are going through counselor training, while others are attending 12 step meetings. They are learning there is no doubt remission could be spiritually oriented.

One cleric states, “I always though those in AA might pray to a “doorknob” as their higher power. I was surprised to find many AA members either have or they are seeking a relationship with God. “Literature supports the notion that clinical experience which encourages patients to surrender control to a power outside themselves (AA’s first three steps) is beneficial.1

Twelve Step programs have gotten a bad rap from those who have never attended meetings or know the story of the 12 step program roots. Preachers are often shocked to find the genesis of AA had deep spiritual roots. So deep in fact the founders had to lighten up a bit in their selling of the concept to addicts to get them to even listen.

Rather than beat the drunk over the head with the Bible, AA members share their experience, strength and hope5 with fervor much like an evangelist. They tout AA attendance is linked to better prognosis when treating addiction.

To create an alliance the addiction community must reach out to clergy with orientation classes on the disease concept and encourage ministers to sit in on 12 step meetings. The olive branch must be extended because psychologists and psychiatrists in particular have been notoriously uninterested when not downright hostile toward religion.2 today however therapist and recovery centers are bridging the gap by offering training and Chaplaincy positions to clergy.

One minister remarked, “The 12 step program is like a walk through the Bible, as it relates to redemption from a problem. The acknowledgment of helplessness, the surrender to a higher power, admitting ones wrongs, and the desire to rebuild relationships and lives.

As to the disease concept, in the argument between the clergy and the addiction community much of it is semantics. No minister would deny the hold addictions have on a person and the impossible task of fighting it alone. Even The American Psychological Association, once wary of anything even vaguely religious, has now published a series of scholarly and clinical volumes on the interface of psychology with spirituality and religion.2 Even in religious circles the pervasiveness of an act that becomes deeply rooted is akin to the disease concept.

Many clerics have gotten the idea the disease concept has eliminated personal responsibility. But one only needs to look at the 12 steps to know the person in recovery has to assume responsibility for their actions. Literature suggests a higher level of religious involvement lowers levels of substance use and problems, both in concurrent measurement and at future times in longitudinal research.2

The key is found in the acknowledging of a higher power, in looking to the outside for inner strength. It is not about looking outside oneself to fix blame. The recovery process via the disease concept does not negate personal responsibility. Once clergy understand that then the gulf between the two schools of thought narrow.

Clinicians should certainly be aware of the importance of spirituality in relation to the recovery process and to those in treatment. In fact this need for more awareness has become increasingly appreciated. As an example, The Joint Commission on Accreditation of Healthcare Organizations now expects patients in alcohol and other substance treatment programs to be queried on their religious orientation as a part of their overall evaluation.

When ministers understand they are actually on the same page with disease issues they can embrace the recovery process and the higher power concept.

The disease issue then is no longer a stumbling block, but rather a stepping-stone to buy into the recovery and 12-step program. It has been found that even among the most compromised of substance abusers studied; spirituality was regarded by them as essential to their recovery.[3]

Lastly the recovery community needs to open its doors to the chaplain concept. The health care industry has long used Chaplains to assist in the care of patients. The National Institute of Health through the Office of Behavioral and Social Science Research recently convened a task force to study the status of the need for research on spirituality and health.[2]

The quickest way to continue to bridge the gap with skeptical clergy is to start a Chaplain program and train the ministers in what they need to know.

A word of caution is urged as some practitioners who incorporate religious practice in their approach may miss out on issues that seem amenable to religious influence but are actually related to other factors such as clinical depression that need medication as well.

As the two sides come together hopefully one will take the ball and create a curriculum for Addiction Chaplain Program. Seminary does not cover the need to know from the recovery community point of view. One possibility is to establish clinical pastoral education in the in patient recovery setting.

Those ministers who are clinical pastoral counselors have most likely either been exposed to the therapeutic concept or are at least open to it but virtue of the type training they have received.

One of the hardest nuts to crack will be the old mainline denominationalist who pastor stoic churches and are dogmatic about their belief system. However the proof is in the pudding.

All it requires is one or two addicts who are in recovery, clean and sober and sitting on the front pew Sunday morning. It is those people who are living out their experience, strength, and hope,[5] the tenets of AA.

One must believe the two sides are closer than ever as each attempts to address the problems of addiction and the millions of dollars it costs and the untold countless lives it spends.

To Carl Jung it was no news that addiction and healthy spirituality were not mutually exclusive, "Spiritus contra spiritum "Jung said of alcoholism: one drives out the other.2

References:

Spirituality in the Treatment of Addictions, Duane F. Reinert, Ph. D., Connections, 2002

Spirituality and Addiction: What Research Is Telling Us, William R. Miller, Ph.D., ICIHS, 2002

The Role of Spirituality in the Prevention and Treatment of Alcohol and Other Substance Addictions, Marc Galanter, M.D., ICIHS, 2002

(4) King James Bible, original 1611

(5) A.A. Big Book, 3rd addition, 1976

(6) Interview, Dr. Dan Chapman, Chaplain BRMC, Early, Texas, 2001

Oh Me of Little Faith

The Emergency Room Miracle of a Two Year Old Boy

I was flipping through the day's mail, "P.J. is on the phone for you Dave". P.J. is the Station Manager for EMS, an advanced life support service contracting with the county.

"Dave, we have a two year old that may have drowned, out on a county road. Units are in route, the dispatcher said it was really bad. They say he was in a septic tank.

As I jumped in my car to head to the ER where the child would be taken, I knew it was bad. I could hear the DPS and Sheriff's patrol units, blocking intersections for the ambulance. Anytime a child dies, everyone takes it personally.

Entering the ER I asked where everyone was, "We're ready a clerk said pointing to a treatment room." Peering inside I saw a full code team ready and waiting. They didn't have to wait long. A Sheriff's Deputy ran in, "they are just rounding the corner".

As I walked out on the ER tarmac, two ambulances pulled in, led by a highway patrolman and a sheriff's officer. I recognized both officers, they have young children themselves.

I helped opened the back door on the unit, and I saw inside, four people including the two paramedics. A fireman had driven the truck in. Another fireman, also a paramedic was helping work the code, while his partner drove Rescue 1 behind them.

I could barely see the child on the stretcher, so very small, so ashen, no sign of life. They wheeled the boy into the trauma room, where the ER staff was waiting, they immediately began.

I walked back outside looking for parents who usually follow an ambulance. In a couple of minutes here came the grandmother of the child along with the young mother, both almost speechless, I could see the look of horror in the mom's eyes.

A social worker/nurse, for the hospital joined us in the family room. We began to explain what was being done in the trauma room. Just a few minutes later a burly man and a younger man entered the family room. I immediately recognized the young man. He was the news director of a local radio station. But he wasn't here for the story; he was the child's uncle.

Let's pray the older man said, and then speaking with the air of authority he began to pray. "I speak to his body in Jesus name, and I command him to live in Jesus name". I immediately identified the prayer style as Charismatic, knowing that these followers spoke much of faith and God's power over the Devil. His prayer continued, "We bind you death in the name of Jesus".

We were all holding hands, the nurse in the circle glanced up at me; she wanted to see my reaction to prayer that seemed a bit strange to her. I winked and slightly nodded as if to say it's ok.

When we finished praying the Grandfather of the child said. "I don't want a negative word spoken in here, not one word at all". I knew their faith tradition believed in not speaking the problem, but praying the solution. I began to mull it over in my mind as to how the beliefs would work in the hospital, at least as a practical matter.

I went back to the trauma room. I counted 12 people working on the child or in a support role. The local on call pediatrician had arrived and was conferring with the ER doc. CPR was still underway. A line had been started (IV) and the tiny patient was being tubed.

I went back to the family room, to report the ER staff was working very hard to revive the boy. "I want to go back in there and pray," the grandfather told me. I slipped into the trauma room and whispered to the ER doc, "ok if the grand dad comes in to pray as long as I keep him back?" I knew the doctor was a Christian and that he would approve the request. He did.

I led the grandfather into the room, and eased him toward the head of the gurney, yet out of the way of the lines, tubes and busy hands. He laid his hands on the child, and began, "In The name of Jesus, you shall live and not die! The prayer continued for several minutes. I touched the grandfather's shoulder, and prayed myself. The ER crew continued to work. Several shifted uneasily. This was a new experience for most of them.

Many of the staff had not been working 10 years ago, when an 8 year old boy died at the ER, as the result of a car- bike accident. The family wanted to pray to raise him from the dead. The ER doc had agreed, by allowing us to take the body to the Chapel for privacy. It allowed the family to practice their faith. And kept out of ear shod from other patients and ER staff. The child didn't come back to life, but it wasn't for any lack of effort, on the part of the family.

Back in the trauma room, no good news. CPR still underway. Gloom on the doctor's faces. I went with him to speak to the anxiously waiting family. Sitting with them, "we are giving him a lot of medicine for his heart, there is no change, and we are still trying. I have to be honest with you, it doesn't look good at all, and if we managed to get him back, well....well, we don't know what he might be like."

Sobs from the mother. The grandfather who accompanied me saying, "What he is saying are just words, they don't have to be true, in the name of Jesus we speak life". Just keep praying the young doctor said, returning to the code in progress. The grandfather and I back in the trauma room. Still no progress.

I went back to the family room. I called the uncle of the child and their pastor into the hall. "Guys someone needs to hear me on this. You need to be prepared if the child does not make it.

I know you don't want anything negative said, but somebody has to be prepared. I have already spoken to the doctor. If they call the code, they know you will want to come in and try to raise him from the dead. It will be ok to do that if you want to.

Back in the trauma room with the granddad. A nurse is checking for a femoral pulse. "I feel something she said". Tears in her eyes. "I think I feel a pulse, but ever so slightly. I glace at the doctor his eyes are transfixed on the cardiac monitor. "Wow". Look at this. A rhythm. The granddad gives a knowing smile. I race to the family room.

"We have a pulse, we have a pulse". The family crying and hugging. "Don't get too excited I said, "Sometimes the medicine causes the heart to beat. We just don't know yet. I turned to leave and the doctor walked into the room. "We do have a pulse. I mean he wasn't responding to anything. We almost quit three times, called the code, but we would want to go a little longer", his voice breaking with emotions. "If he continues this, I'm going to call the Children's Hospital and see if they will take him.

I had seen in the hall earlier, a deputy sheriff who would take a report, a state trooper who escorted the ambulance, and a Justice of the Peace. In Texas if there is no Coroner in a county, then the J.P. determines the cause of death. All their eyes wide. "You may not need me, the Judge inquires?" "That's right Judge we may not."

Child trying to breathe a bit on its own. "I have talked to the Children's Hospital, there are going to find a bed", the doc tells us.

People still praying in the family room, and the ever vigilant granddad back in the trauma room. "Chaplain tell them to worship now, to praise now, that's what they can do now. But run any negative person out of there".

Vitals are improving; the warming blankets are bringing up the body temperature. Wow. I visited with the family and told them how happy I was for them. I got the cell phone number from several family members I knew. "They are going to fly him I said. Either on our helicopter or they will request Teddy Bear Air a fixed wing to come get him. They have the pediatric ICU nurses aboard."

Saying my goodbyes for now, leaving the social worker/nurse with the family. I headed back out.

I called all the responding agencies to give them the good news. There had been a save. A miracle in ER. What had just happened? I had always heard that if you were going to die, drowning stood the best chance of resuscitation. I'm an EMT myself. I remembered in class, "the cold water slows down the metabolism" The organs are preserved.

Battling in my own mind. "Was it prayer, or was it just the cold water?" I have been a police Chaplain more than 15 years and a hospital Chaplain for almost 20. I had seen so many things. I am a believer, a strong Christian. Why had I experienced some trouble with the prayers of the family? Fortunately, I remembered it's all about them! This is not about me!

Talking to a ward clerk, "Dave while they were working the code the ER doc told them the story of the little boy who died in the collapse of the sand pit. Do you remember that"? I remembered it well.

A young boy about 10 years old was playing in a rural area and didn't return home. Parents went looking and found him buried in a sand pile. Not breathing, no pulse. They call 911, dad giving CPR.

Rushed by ambulance. Code in progress. At the ER, working the code, an hour or more passes. Nothing worked. Sadly the doctor called the code. Time of death, 8:04. Walking with the Chaplain to tell the parents. Very bad news, your son didn't make it, he is dead. We tried everything.

Back in the trauma room a young nurse starting to clean up. She is thinking, "I had always heard you weren't dead, until you were "warm" and dead." She started putting warm blankets on the boy. Still cleaning up. What was that? Movement she thought, out of the corner of her eye. Looking," Good Lord", a finger moved. Rushing to where the doctor, Chaplain and family were, He's alive, he moved, I think he is alive". Wow.

The tech told me, "Dave after he told that story, there was new life, new energy in that trauma room. Let's not quit, keep working the code."

Later that evening, on my way to do a debriefing (CISD) at the EMS station, I called the child's uncle. "Bryan, how is he doing? Better? Really? Responding to painful stimuli? Great. Vitals good, body temp coming up? Excellent! Yes I'm there now. Sure I'll tell them."

Sitting down for the debriefing. "Folks there is good news. They made it to Children's Hospital. He is doing better".

Walking out in the cool night air, getting in my car to head home. What a day. In the debriefing several talked about the prayers they heard. About the almost shouting of life back into the body. We talked about different faith traditions. Just because something is new, or loud for that matter, doesn't make it wrong.

Was it just the cold water someone asked? But we have pulled kids from cold water before and they didn't survive. What about the story of the other child who came back, the one told in the trauma room. No cold water there. What kept the doctors from calling the code, not once or twice, but deciding a third time to keep working on the child.

Faith is a funny thing. The Bible talks about faith, as small as a mustard seed. And without faith, it's impossible to please God.

There is a lot to read about faith. One thing is for sure. The family of this little boy. They had faith. That kind of faith that moves mountains"

I was reminded of a scripture in Hebrews:

Heb 11:1-3

11:1 Now faith is the substance of things hoped for, the evidence of things not seen.

2 For by it the elders obtained a good report. 3 Through faith we understand that the worlds were framed by the word of God, so that things which are seen were not made of things which do appear. KJV

One thing is for sure, if I was a betting man, I would lay you odds. There was not a person working in that trauma room, that didn't say their prayers that night. Maybe some, even for the very first time.

NATIONAL POLICE WEEK

Again this year the Police Chaplains are distributing "Blue Ribbons" from the Concerns of Police Survivors (COPS).

May 15th is POLICE MEMORIAL DAY in hour of our fallen brothers and sisters of law enforcement.

Please take a Blue Ribbon and attach it to your antenna especially on May 15th.

We appreciate each of you, along with our civilian employees.

Thank you for all you do.

David J. Fair
Director of Chaplain Services

Author
Dave Fair Served at Ground Zero Following 911

Police chaplains tend to hearts, minds and souls

For most Americans, they were galvanizing events witnessed in the blue flicker of televised reality horror: Killeen… Waco… Oklahoma City… the World Trade Center… the Columbia.

For professionals who tend disaster detail, such calamities can be numbing sensory assaults. Sounds, smells, tastes, feelings and graphic images absorbed at the scene can haunt and persist, branded on the brain, buried in shallow skin.

That's when the call goes out for Dr. David J. (Dave) Fair. The Brownwood, Texas police chaplain is a renowned crisis intervention and stress management specialist for emergency responders. To Dr. Fair, the primary job of a police chaplain, in a nutshell, is to provide "psychological first aid."

Professionals who ply the front lines of unnatural disasters can become collateral victims, overwhelmed by a psychic tsunami. "It begins eating you from the inside out," says Dr. Fair, who has counseled safety officials involved in some of our nation's most prominent recent tragedies. He is a founding principal of the Crisis Response Chaplains Service, a non-profit organization "providing psychological services, consultation and pastoral care for all public safety personnel and their families."

"Traumatic stress is a normal reaction to an abnormal situation," he continues. "It normally self corrects, over time, with what we call 'ventilate and validate.' We simply ask a person some directed questions and let them vent their thoughts, feelings and emotions. We validate those feelings; reassure them that any person going through that type of situation would feel the same way. Sometimes, though, people get stuck. If they're stuck for over thirty days, it can become a psychological diagnosis of post-traumatic stress disorder."

That's why police chaplains, and their use of interventional processes like Critical Incident Stress Debriefing (CISD), are such valuable assets to public agencies in today's fast-paced, stress-laced culture. Also a licensed EMT, Dr. Fair fully grasps the "first aid" analogy. Just as interventional medical first aid potentially averts residual injuries, psychological first aid can help prevent deeper, lingering psychological scars.

For more information on starting a law enforcement Chaplain program
Contact
The International Conference of Police Chaplains at their website

To contact Dave Fair
Or to learn more about specialized Chaplain Programs see

www.crisis-chaplain.org

chaplaindfair@hotmail.com

The articles, forms, news reports, photos, and references were prepared, edited, or revised by the author. All journal and magazine articles are original works by Dave Fair. Most have been printed elsewhere. If per chance we have quoted you, revamped an idea we read or heard, used information from other works, and failed to credit you, let us know and we will give you credit in a future volume. Chaplains work together, share ideas, and help one another. Anything we included in this book is intended for use by all Chaplains. Share the information and use it to **THE GLORY OF GOD**

www.ingramcontent.com/pod-product-compliance
Ingram Content Group UK Ltd.
Pitfield, Milton Keynes, MK11 3LW, UK
UKHW041946190726
13854UKWH00004B/1814

9 781411 627369